299.5  W9-AKD-381
Hartz, Paula
Daoism

$40.00
ocn243845488
3rd ed.   08/05/2009

WORLD RELIGIONS
DAOISM
THIRD EDITION

WORLD RELIGIONS

African Traditional Religion
Baha'i Faith
Buddhism
Catholicism & Orthodox Christianity
Confucianism
Daoism
Hinduism
Islam
Judaism
Native American Religions
Protestantism
Shinto
Sikhism
Zoroastrianism

WORLD RELIGIONS
DAOISM
THIRD EDITION

by
Paula R. Hartz
Series Editors: Joanne O'Brien and Martin Palmer

CHELSEA HOUSE
PUBLISHERS
An imprint of Infobase Publishing

Daoism, Third Edition

Chelsea House
An imprint of Infobase Publishing
132 West 31st Street
New York NY 10001

CIP Library of Congress Cataloging-in-Publication Data
Hartz, Paula.
  Daoism / by Paula R. Hartz. — 3rd ed.
    p. cm. — (World religions)
  Includes bibliographical references and index.
  ISBN 978-1-60413-115-4
  1. Taoism—Juvenile literature. I. Title. II. Series.
  BL1920.H37 2009
  299.5'14—dc22

       2008035809

Chelsea House books are available at special discounts when purchased in bulk quantities for businesses, associations, institutions, or sales promotions. Please call our Special Sales Department in New York at (212) 967-8800 or (800) 322-8755.

You can find Chelsea House on the World Wide Web at http://www.chelseahouse.com

This book was produced for Chelsea House by Bender Richardson White, Uxbridge, U.K.
Project Editor: Lionel Bender
Text Editor: Ronne Randall
Designer: Ben White
Picture Researchers: Joanne O'Brien and Kim Richardson
Maps and symbols: Stefan Chabluk

Printed in China

CP BRW 10 9 8 7 6 5 4 3 2 1
This book is printed on acid-free paper.

All links and Web addresses were checked and verified to be correct at the time of publication. Because of the dynamic nature of the Web, some addresses and links may have changed since publication and may no longer be valid.

CONTENTS

PREFACE

Almost from the start of civilization, more than 10,000 years ago, religion has shaped human history. Today, more than half the world's population practice a major religion or indigenous spiritual tradition. In many 21st-century societies, including the United States, religion still shapes people's lives and plays a key role in politics and culture. And in societies throughout the world increasing ethnic and cultural diversity has led to a variety of religions being practiced side-by-side. This makes it vital that we understand as much as we can about the world's religions.

The World Religions series, of which this book is a part, sets out to achieve this aim. It is written and designed to appeal to both students and general readers. The books offer clear, accessible overviews of the major religious traditions and institutions of our time. Each volume in the series describes where a particular religion is practiced, its origins and history, its central beliefs and important rituals, and its contributions to world civilization. Carefully chosen photographs complement the text, and sidebars, a map, fact file, glossary, bibliography, and an index are included to help readers gain a more complete understanding of the subject at hand.

These books will help clarify what religion is all about and reveal both the similarities and differences in the great spiritual traditions practiced around the world today.

Area where Daoism is a major influence

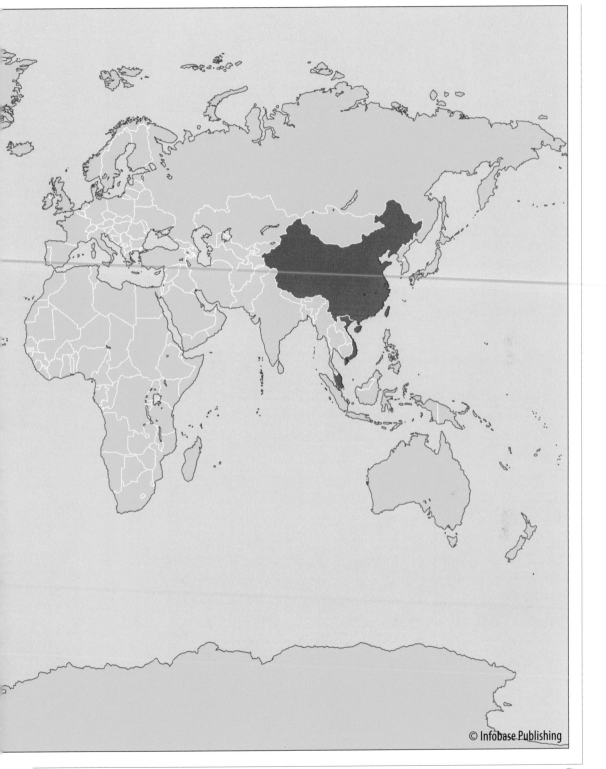

© Infobase Publishing

CHAPTER 1

INTRODUCTION: THE MODERN DAOIST WORLD

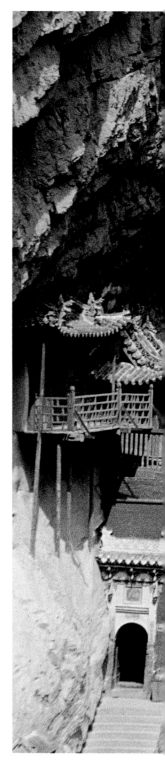

aoism (pronounced DOW-ism) is one of the two great philosophical and religious traditions that originated in China. The other religion native to China is Confucianism. Both Daoism and Confucianism began at about the same time, around the sixth century B.C.E. or between 500 and 400 B.C.E. China's third great tradition, Buddhism, came to China from India around the second century C.E. Together these three faiths have shaped Chinese life and thought for nearly 2,500 years.

Wherever the Chinese people have gone they have taken Daoism with them. Thus elements of Daoism appear in many of the countries that came under Chinese influence over the centuries—countries such as Korea, Vietnam, and Japan—and in the Chinese sections of Western cities in Europe, Canada, and the United States. Daoism has also had a strong influence on Chinese literature and on the technique and subject matter of Chinese art. The People's Republic of China is officially atheist (believes that there is no deity), so it is hard to know how many of its people are Daoists but it is estimated that hundreds of millions of peo-

The Hanging Temple on northern Heng Shan, one of the five sacred mountains of Daoism. Located in Shanxi Province, the Hanging Temple was built in the Northern Wei dynasty (386–534 C.E.) and has been a site of Daoist pilgrimage for many centuries.

ple practice elements of Daoism. Many people would not define themselves as being a Daoist, because they will use elements of Daoism and Buddhism at different stages of their lives. However, followers of Traditional Chinese religion—which is largely Daoist—are the majority of believers in China today. Since the Chinese government now allows people to practice religion again, many Daoist temples have been restored and reopened, and Daoism is on the rise.

DAO

To a reader of Chinese a single character can convey many shades of meaning. According to its use a character can be a noun, a verb, or an adjective. Used as a noun the word *dao* is usually translated as "path" or "way," but *dao* has other meanings also: a way of doing things, the way of the universe, or the basic way of life that Daoists follow. To Daoists the written character for *dao* symbolizes Dao as an inner way as well as an outward path.

A single Chinese character may indeed have many different meanings. However each part of that character may also have a meaning of its own. For example, the character for *dao* is a combination of two characters that represent the words "head" and "foot." The character for *foot* suggests the idea of a person's direction or path. The character for *head* suggests the idea of conscious choice. But *head* also suggests a beginning, and *foot* an ending. Thus the character for *dao* also conveys the continuing course of the universe, the circle of heaven and earth. Finally, the character for *dao* demonstrates the Daoist idea that the eternal Dao is both moving and unmoving. The "head" in the character represents the beginning—the source of all things—or Dao itself, which never moves or changes; the "foot" is the movement on the path.

道

dao

首

head

foot

WHAT IS DAOISM?

When used as a noun in Chinese, the word *dao* means "the way." Simply put, the way is understood to mean the way of nature. Daoists see the cycles of nature and the constant change in the natural world as earthly signs of a great and universal force. They call this unseen force Dao.

For some Dao is the Ultimate Reality, a presence that existed before the universe was formed and that continues to guide the world and everything in it. Dao is sometimes identified as the Mother, or the source of all things. However, that source is not a god or a supreme being, for unlike Christianity, Islam, and Judaism, Daoism is not monotheistic. Its followers do not worship one god; practitioners focus instead on coming into harmony with Dao. The great Daoist masters were men who taught or wrote about Dao, or who commented on the Daoist writings of others. Daoists look to the works of those masters, such as Laozi of the sixth century B.C.E. and Zhuangzi of the fourth century B.C.E., to help them find "the way."

Daoists say that the Dao that can be expressed in words is not the real or "eternal" Dao. Masters and writers can help to point the way, but each person must find his or her own Dao.

Learned, but Not Taught

According to the Daoist masters, Dao can be learned, but it cannot be taught.

Look, and it can't be seen. Listen, and it can't be heard. Reach, and it can't be grasped . . . You can't know it, but you can be it, at ease in your own life.

(In Stephen Mitchell, *Tao Te Ching: A New English Version*.)

INNER HARMONY

Daoism reaches not only into the intellectual and spiritual lives of its followers, but also into their physical life. Daoists see the physical body as a kind of microcosm, or miniature model, of the universe. Natural forces create the energy of life and their interaction affects the health of the individual. Daoists ask: How can a person be in harmony with the universe if his or her body is not in harmony with itself? Thus to a Daoist the way in which someone treats his or her body is as important as what that person thinks, believes, or does in relation to others.

A Chinese herbalist's shop in Hong Kong. Many Chinese families rely on the herbal medicines that were developed by Daoist alchemists and herbalists in the early centuries of the common era. Chinese herbal remedies are also popular in the West and are increasingly used by many non-Chinese people.

Daoists believe that a healthy body is a necessary first step to achieving a lofty spiritual state. Thus Daoism has long been associated with certain medicinal and nutritional practices. Many of the ideas and practices that Westerners think of as Chinese or Asian are in fact Daoist. For example acupressure and acupuncture, Eastern medical arts that in the past few years have been the subject of study in Western medicine, were developed by Daoist masters and have been in use for centuries.

DIET AND EXERCISE

Daoist masters have recorded the medicinal uses of thousands of plants—trees, herbs, flowers, fruits, and fungi—and have studied nutrition. The masters recommend a prudent, balanced diet to maintain health and to promote longevity. Daoist recommendations on diet are quite different, however, from the dietary laws of religions such as Judaism and Hinduism, which ask their followers to abstain from certain foods as part of their religious observance. Daoists forbid nothing, recommending only that substances harmful to the body, such as an excess of alcohol, be avoided and that everything else be eaten and drunk in a balanced, sensible, healthful way. To the Daoist, for example, broccoli is a good food but a diet that consists only of broccoli is not good because it is not balanced, and balance is the Daoist way.

In addition to a healthful diet, exercise is an integral part of Daoist practice. According to legend an early Daoist master named Zhang Sanfeng watched the movements of birds and animals and sought to copy them as a way of getting closer to the natural state. He became known as the founder of Taijiquan (*tai chi chuan*), the ancient form of Chinese exercise. Taiji exercises are used to control *qi (chi)*, or "breath," an essential element of human existence, which for Daoists is the center of spiritual, emotional, and physical health. The stretching, bending, and flexing exercises embody the natural *qi* of the animals and dispel the physical tensions that keep people from finding inner peace and being in touch with Dao.

EXISTING AS NATURE DOES

Meditation is often associated with Buddhism and other faiths from India; but long before Buddhism came to China Daoists were using a form of meditation to help them come into harmony with the ultimate reality of the universe. The concept of *wuwei*, or "nondoing," is central to Daoist meditation. It is the practice of quietism—of letting go of all worldly thought and action so that Dao may enter. The phrase *wei wuwei* literally means "to do without doing," or "to act without action," but this literal translation does not express the complete meaning. The concept of *wuwei* more closely suggests a way of existing without conscious effort, as nature does.

ACHIEVING IMMORTALITY

Daoists believe that time spent in meditation prolongs life. In Daoist belief longevity is important, because the longer one lives the greater one's chances are of achieving perfect harmony with Dao. The perfect person might hope to become immortal and rise to heaven—not just in spirit but physically as well. A number of legendary and historical people are believed to have reached this immortal state called *xian*. Worshippers ask these immortals of Daoism to help them, much as some Christians ask saints for help.

The immortals of Daoism include emperors, Daoist masters, heroes of battle, and ordinary people who have attained this exalted condition through suffering, heroic deeds, or service to others. Daoists continue to strive toward *xian,* oneness with the universe, perfecting their bodies as well as their minds.

THREE TEACHINGS INTO ONE

Over the centuries the threads of Confucianism, Buddhism, and Daoism have become intertwined, each absorbing aspects of the others. As the Chinese say, "The three teachings flow into one." This blending of traditions is consistent with the Asian approach to religion, which allows for believing in more than one truth. Thus many people who consider themselves Chinese Buddhists or Confucianists, as well as many agnostics—people who claim that no one can know whether a god exists but who do not deny the possibility of that existence—also practice aspects of Daoism. Such practice is possible because the traditions do not conflict. Rather they complement one another.

YIN AND YANG

In all, Daoists seek balance and harmony in their lives. In Chinese thought yin, "the shady side of the hill," cannot exist without yang, "the sunny side." To have one it is necessary to have the other. Yin is passive; yang is active. Yin is cool; yang is warm. Yin is night; yang is day. Yin is female; yang is male. Daoism celebrates yin, the femaleness of the universe, in which quiet and "letting be" are more fruitful than strife and direct action.

Daoist priests reading from sacred texts as they perform the daily temple ritual in a Chinese temple.

Daoists have never made an attempt to spread their religion. Travelers and wanderers, but never missionaries, they do not visit other countries to win converts. Daoist masters prefer to let students come to them and to counsel them one on one. Many early masters did gather followers, however, and a number of sects resulted. Daoists tend to see the differing interpretations of their beliefs as part of the infinite variety of the universe rather than as right or wrong. Over the centuries Daoism has had many masters and many interpretations.

Like Buddhism, Daoism has different levels. In its purest form it can be the basis for a life of contemplation and prayer. However it also addresses the concerns of ordinary people, offering calm and inner peace, a way to health and long life, and forgiveness of sin through rituals and good works. Fundamental to Daoism is the concept of yin and yang, the interaction between opposite forces in nature.

Drawing of an imaginary meeting between Confucius, Buddha, and Laozi (accompanied by their attendants), representing the three great religious traditions of China. The Buddha lived in India at a slightly earlier period and would not have met Confucius or Laozi, although meetings between Confucius and Laozi have been recorded in Chinese sources. Such a meeting may have taken place although there is no historical evidence.

DAOISM AND THE THREE TRADITIONS

Daoism shares with Confucianism and Buddhism many of the attributes that make them different from Western religions. Like Buddhists and Confucianists, Daoists do not attend regularly scheduled worship services or make statements of faith. There is no specific creed to which they must subscribe. While there are many traditional observances and rituals, there are none in which a follower must participate in order to be a Daoist.

Unlike followers of Christianity or Islam or Judaism, Daoists, Buddhists, and Confucianists do not believe in a supreme being or in the immortality of the soul. Believers in Western traditions are concerned with the love of people for God, but religion in China has long concerned itself with practical moral behavior and self-improvement. Like the other "great truths," Daoism provides guidance for living a moral life and attempts to explain the place of human beings in the natural universe. Some of Daoism's practices for health and serenity attract followers of their own.

As a result, Daoism accommodates many points of view and practices. Daoist monks and nuns may retreat from the world and live in monasteries, trying to achieve spiritual perfection and become one with Dao. Daoist priests may live and work among the people, performing ancient rituals for health, prosperity, and redemption from sin. Some individuals may follow a particular Daoist practice such as Taijiquan or meditation, or they may pursue an interest in Chinese medicine. Others may follow the religious rituals of Daoism in their homes, lighting incense to the spirits of their ancestors and the Daoist gods. All of these people consider themselves Daoists. They are all part of the living religion, examples of its vitality and strength.

CHAPTER 2

THE ORIGINS AND EARLY HISTORY OF DAOISM

Scholars believe that the core ideas of Daoism began as a way of thinking around the sixth century B.C.E. However the roots of Daoist thought are much older than that. It can be argued they are as old as the oldest legends and beliefs of the Chinese people. For many Daoist believers Daoism can be traced to the great and wise ruler Huangdi, also known as the Yellow Emperor.

Huangdi was one of several legendary emperors who lived before recorded history. Stories about him appear in many ancient sources. He is said to have ruled from 2696 to 2598 B.C.E., almost 100 years.

According to legend, in the 19th year of his reign Huangdi traveled into the mountains to consult a very old and wise hermit (one who lives in solitude) about the secret of life. At first the

The Eight Immortals, part of the Daoist pantheon of gods, are among the most popular Chinese deities and are believed to help those in need, sometimes coming in disguise. The Eight Immortals are often the subject of paintings, sculptures, and legends that reveal their human characteristics as well as their supernatural powers.

hermit would not answer Huangdi's questions. Then Huangdi succeeded in his quest and he came away with great knowledge—knowledge that he applied to many areas of life and government. Thus Huangdi is revered not only for having been a wise and just emperor but also for having been the first to diagnose and cure many diseases, to use magic to tame wild animals, and to use military strategy effectively.

The hermit explained to Huangdi that he had lived to be 1,200 years old by dwelling in Dao, or in harmony with the universe. Huangdi adopted the hermit's principles and at the end of his glorious 99-year reign he rode off to heaven on the back of a dragon and thus became immortal.

This legend expresses a longing that has existed since before recorded time. Even then people were searching for the right way to live so that they too might enjoy endless life. One "way" came to be called Daoism.

THE GOLDEN AGE OF PHILOSOPHY

The first ruling dynasty (family) of record was the Shang dynasty, which began around 1700 B.C.E. The records describe cities, social classes, a calendar, and an organized government. In 1027 B.C.E., after approximately 700 years of Shang rule, the Zhou (Chou) dynasty came into power. The Zhou rulers remained in charge for almost 800 years.

The Zhou dynasty began in a dynamic way. Written laws were developed, money came into use, and farming took a giant step forward with the invention of an iron plow. However after several hundred years widespread political corruption and disorder began to take over. The people began to long for the simpler, happier life of ancient times. They wanted direction, and to find it they turned to philosophers and sages—the great thinkers and writers of the age. This period became known as the Golden Age of Philosophy, which would last until the middle of the 5th century B.C.E. It produced several men whose works have endured over the centuries and on whose thoughts and teachings the great religious traditions of China are based.

A dragon carved on the roof of a Daoist temple. In Chinese culture, this mythical creature is believed to have fantastic powers and is often associated with great strength and wisdom.

Ethical Behavior

Confucius, one of the great thinkers of the Golden Age (551–479 B.C.E.) taught principles of moral behavior. He felt that a person who lived by his rules would develop the habit of ethical behavior. Eventually this behavior would become deeply ingrained in one's personality. The person who followed his principles would thus achieve virtue.

CONFUCIUS

One of the great thinkers of the Golden Age was Confucius, who was born around 551 B.C.E. Confucius believed that the cure for the problems of society was moral, ethical behavior. He traveled from court to court trying to convince rulers to govern according to his plan.

Confucius rejected all that was violent, disorderly, strange, or supernatural. His teachings recommended respect for the gods but he concentrated on relationships between people. He set rules for all levels and types of relationships: the equality of friend to friend and the hierarchical relationship between parent and child, ruler and subject, husband and wife, and older and younger siblings. His rules stressed loyalty, decency, trustworthiness, and propriety.

THE IDEAL SOCIETY

The Confucian ideal society was one in which the emperor cared for his subjects as a loving father would, and his subjects obeyed as loving children; one in which younger would obey older and wiser, women would obey men and all would live in harmony in a family.

Confucius advised people to respect the good example of others, to behave properly toward all, and to be prudent and follow the middle course. "The cautious seldom make mistakes," he said. He also stressed the importance of studying the Classics, books that summarized the wisdom and thought of China. He suggested that emperors hire scholars to study the works of the

THE ANALECTS

The followers of Confucius gathered all his sayings and parables—simple stories that illustrate a moral—in a work known as the *Analects*. Confucianism, as the tradition that came from the teachings of Confucius was called, stressed rules of conduct and etiquette. It promoted ritual as the way to harmony between people and heaven; it promoted rules of behavior to create harmony between individuals and within society at large.

A statue of Confucius in the Temple of Confucius in Suzhou, Jiangsu Province, China.

With their ancient farming culture many Chinese felt closer to the forces of nature than to the problems of government. Popular religious practice reflected this connection. People honored their ancestors, local gods, the gods of the heavens, and the gods of the earth. They believed that the spirits of great leaders continued to exist and that their spiritual powers could be called upon. Close observation of nature had convinced the people that there was a pattern in the universe and an unseen, perhaps unknowable, force behind it.

great thinkers in Chinese history. The scholars would then be able to convey their accumulated wisdom to the emperors and their courts. In this way all that was good, fitting, and proper in Chinese tradition would become integrated with current society.

A FRAMEWORK FOR LIVING

Confucianism, as the tradition that came from the teachings of Confucius was called, appealed to the practical minds and common sense of the Chinese people. In China's bustling, crowded cities and palaces, it provided a framework within which the people could structure their lives and conduct business and government.

Confucianism was a yardstick by which to measure one's own conduct and the conduct of others, a standard for choosing officials and business associates. In times of war and government corruption it was a clear path to follow. It won many adherents.

Not everyone agreed with the ideas of Confucius, however. Some people felt that Confucianism focused too much on society and government and not enough on the relationship of people to the natural world. Its emphasis on rules of conduct and the ethical treatment of others in society did not satisfy people's spiritual needs in understanding the meaning of life and death nor was it in keeping with many of the existing beliefs of those who lived close to the earth.

LAOZI

Like the Yellow Emperor centuries before him, the man on whose teachings Daoism is based is semilegendary. No one is really sure whether or not he existed. It has been suggested that he was not one person but a composite of many wise men of his time. Still, the earliest history of China, written around the second century B.C.E., includes a biographical sketch of this man. It says that his name was Li Ehr and that he was Confucius's contemporary, although slightly older than Confucius.

The steep rock faces of Hua Shan, a sacred mountain in Shaanxi Province. Many Daoist sages and hermits sought reflection and union with the Dao in the temples and caves on this sacred mountain.

Meeting a Dragon

After meeting Daoist master Laozi, the great Chinese thinker Confucius remarked, "I know that birds can fly and fish can swim and beasts can run. Snares can be set for things that run, nets for those that swim, and arrows for whatever flies. But dragons! I shall never know how they ride wind and cloud up into the sky. Today I saw Laozi. What a dragon!"

Little is known about his life. According to tradition he worked as the archivist in the royal palace in Luoyang, the capital of the Zhou dynasty. There he became known as Laozi (Lao Tzu), which is a title meaning "The Old Master."

MEETING CONFUCIUS

According to tradition Laozi grew in wisdom during his lifetime and many people consulted him on the questions of religion and politics. A source written some 200 years after Laozi's lifetime reveals the details of a meeting between Laozi and Confucius in Luoyang.

Laozi was known for his virtue and his wise teachings, but he was apparently impatient with fools and sharp-tongued people. He was also impatient with Confucius's practical ways and challenged the belief that knowledge and learning, not to mention a code of behavior, would help people improve. People, he suggested, were born good and needed nothing to keep them that way except to be left alone. Certainly there was no point, he felt, in studying the works of past masters. "All the men of which you speak have long since moldered away to their bones," Laozi snapped to Confucius. "Give up your proud airs, your many wishes, mannerisms, and extravagant claims. They won't do you any good! That's all I have to tell you."

WITHDRAWAL TO THE MOUNTAINS

Laozi worked in the royal archives of the Zhou court until he was over 90 years old. By that time the dynasty was in its decline. Tired of government work, he decided to leave the province. As he traveled through a mountain pass, riding on a water buffalo, he was recognized by a border guard. The guard was distressed to think that the wisdom of this great sage would be lost to the kingdom forever. He asked Laozi to record his wise thoughts before leaving the province.

This stone carving depicts Laozi riding a buffalo toward the Gateway to the West. Before he left the province where he taught and worked, he stopped to write what became the greatest Daoist classic—the *Daodejing*.

According to the legendary story Laozi sat down then and there and wrote out a little manuscript, only 5,000 Chinese characters long. He gave it to the guard; then he left the province and was not heard from again. The manuscript he left behind is known as the *Laozi,* or, more commonly, the *Daodejing (Tao Te Ching),* "The Book of the Way and Its Power."

THE *DAODEJING*

The *Daodejing* is a collection of 81 short chapters. Scholars today feel that the *Daodejing* is not the work of one person but rather a collection of the works of many people, gathered over a period of time, probably during the fourth century B.C.E., about 200 years after Laozi's lifetime. Still, the *Daodejing,* with its philosophical beliefs, is traditionally attributed to Laozi.

Whether the *Daodejing* is the work of one or of many, certainly its writer or writers were drawing on a tradition already thousands of years old when the book was created. The poems are tightly written in a very few words, and people have discussed and debated their meanings for centuries, much as they do the meaning and relevance of the writings in the Judeo-Christian Bible.

Many of the poems are in effect advice on how to rule, but not in the way people might expect a ruler would be advised. The advice is surprising in some ways. For example instead of saying, "Be strong; rule with a firm hand," Laozi counsels, "Be weak; let things alone." He counsels humility and inaction, saying that rulers who interfere in the lives of the people are asking for trouble.

Sometimes the statements in the *Daodejing* are expressed in paradoxes—statements that seem to contradict themselves. For example:

Mixed Reactions

At first glance statements about mastery being achieved through inaction may seem contradictory. How can a ruler rule without ruling? Yet Laozi's ideas are consistent. What is low cannot fall, and what bends does not break. He suggests handling small problems before they become big ones; he points out that by rushing, people make mistakes that are hard to undo. "The Dao," Laozi says, "is always at ease. It overcomes without competing, answers without speaking a word, arrives without being summoned, accomplishes without a plan."

True mastery can be gained
by letting things go their own way.
It can't be gained by interfering.

And later:

Seeing into darkness is clarity.
Knowing how to yield is strength.
(In Stephen Mitchell, *Tao Te Ching:*
A New English Version.)

SEEKING THE DAO

Like water feeding the earth Dao gives birth to and nourishes everything but makes no claim to importance. Like water the wise person will work without calling attention to himself or herself, will do what is right and fair, and will become attuned to the nature of things. That person will understand Dao.

People must learn to seek Dao, which is unimportant in the sense that it is not noticeable—it cannot be seen or experienced through the senses. According to Laozi people become separated from Dao when the wrong things become important to them, such as power, success, and learning. In saying this, he was challenging the norms of Confucianiam and imperial thinking for whom these very things were central. When people abandon those things they will be enriched in spirit. Ambition and contention block "quietism" and the ability to open oneself to unity with Dao.

The *Daodejing* was written as an aid to wisdom and leadership. In addition to the passages on how to live and how to find Dao, it contained many sections on how to govern. Thus the first people who followed Laozi's teachings were mainly those from the ruling families, those who had access to education. However those who adopted Laozi's teachings did so as a personal philosophy,

THE NOURISHING FORCE

According to Dao master Laozi, Dao teaches the unimportance of importance. Water takes the low, or unimportant, path as it seeps into the ground. Unnoticed, it is the nourishing force that sustains plants, people, and animals. The lower it sinks the more truly important it is. Laozi says:

The supreme good is like water,
Which nourishes all things without trying to.
It is content to take the low places that people disdain.
Thus it is like the Dao.

(In Stephen Mitchell, *Tao Te Ching: A New English Version*.)

ZHUANGZI'S DREAM

Zhuangzi (Zhuang Zi or Zhuang Zhou), a Daoist master, was known for the wit with which he mocked those who took themselves too seriously. In the great scheme of things, he suggests, people are not terribly important, an idea that he illustrates with an autobiographical anecdote in the *Zhuangzi*:

"Once upon a time, I Zhuang Zi, dreamt that I was a butterfly, flitting around enjoying myself. I had no idea I was Zhuang Zi. Then suddenly I woke up and was Zhuang Zi again. But I could not tell, had I been Zhuang Zi dreaming I was a butterfly, or a butterfly dreaming I was now Zhuang Zi?"

(In Martin Palmer and Elizabeth Breuilly, *The Book of Chuang Tzu*.)

A butterfly feeding from a summer flower.

which they practiced privately. They did not pursue the general learning, power, and knowledge of the past that are central to Confucianism.

ZHUANGZI

About two centuries after Laozi another great Daoist master emerged. His name was Zhuangzi (Zhuang Zhou or Chuang Tzu) and he lived from about 369 to 286 B.C.E. He became known as the next great Daoist sage and one of the great literary figures of Chinese history. The *Zhuangzi,* the collection of the works of Master Zhuang, was the first Chinese work to present a philosophy of life that ordinary people could understand and follow for themselves.

Like the *Daodejing,* the *Zhuangzi* may have been written by more than one person or even collected by others after Zhuangzi's death. Nevertheless tradition has it that the works in the book are his. Zhuangzi was a scholar who had studied the works of Laozi. He wrote essays, stories, and parables to illustrate and explain Laozi's teachings to others. Zhuangzi's message is much like that of Laozi, but his style is very different. Instead of short, compact sayings about life and its meaning, Zhuangzi wrote chatty stories that people could relate to easily. His pages illustrate the sayings of Laozi with characters who not only are kings and sages but also are ordinary Chinese working-class potters and meat cutters.

In his writings, Zhuangzi rejected political and social concerns. He believed that living within society made people forget Dao, or the ultimate reality. Society, he suggested, caused people to become

Wuwei, or "Nondoing"

The philosophy of nondoing does not mean withdrawing from action but rather performing a higher kind of action: action in accord with Dao, action that respects the nature of all things. Zhuangzi explained it this way:

Heaven and Earth have great beauty but no words.
The four seasons follow their regular path but do not debate it.
All forms of life have their own distinct natures but do not discuss them.
The sage looks at the beauties of Heaven and Earth and comprehends the principle behind all life.
So the perfect man does without doing And the great sage imitates nothing,
For, as we say, they have glimpsed Heaven and Earth.

(In Martin Palmer and Elizabeth Breuilly, *The Book of Chuang Tzu.*)

In a time when Confucian scholar-officials were finding favor in the emperor's court, Zhuangzi remained cheerfully scornful of government. He was once asked if he would become prime minister of Chu, one of the Chinese kingdoms. He said:

"I hear that in Chu there is a sacred tortoise which died 3,000 years ago. The king keeps this in his ancestral temple, wrapped and enclosed. Tell me, would this tortoise have wanted to die and leave his shell to be venerated?

Or would he rather have lived and continued to crawl about in the mud?"

The two senior officials said,

"It would rather have lived and continued to crawl about in the mud." Zhuang Zi said, *"Shove off, then! I will continue to crawl about in the mud!"*

(In Martin Palmer and Elizabeth Breuilly, *The Book of Chuang Tzu*.)

A giant tortoise feeding. Zhuangzi used many different stories to illustrate his beliefs and teachings including the story of a sacred tortoise.

For Daoist master Zhuangzi, being true to the Dao was to be true to your inner nature. Here is his tale of a master carver who sought harmony with the universe, and the ultimate reality of the Dao, before beginning his work with the wood. The master carver came to achieve mastery of his art by ignoring all thought of gain or praise or even of his own skill:

Woodcarver Ching carved a piece of wood to form a bell support, and those who saw it were astonished because it looked as if ghosts or spirits had done it. The Marquis of Lu saw it and asked, "Where does your art come from?" "I am just a woodcarver," Ching replied. "How could I have 'art'? One thing is certain, though, that when I carve a bell support, I do not allow it to exhaust my original breath (qi), so I take care to calm my heart. After I have fasted for three days, I give no thought to praise, reward, titles or income. After I have fasted for five days I give no thought to glory or blame, to skill or stupidity. After I have fasted for seven days, I am so still that I forget whether I have four limbs and a body. By then the Duke and his court have ceased to exist as far as I am concerned. All my energy is focused and external concerns have gone. After that I depart and enter the mountain forest, and explore the Heavenly innate nature of the trees;

once I find one with a perfect shape, I can see for certain the possibility of a bell support and I set my hand to the task; if I cannot see the possibility, I leave it be. By so doing I harmonize the Heavenly with Heaven, and perhaps this is why it is thought that my carvings are done by spirits!"

(In Martin Palmer and Elizabeth Breuilly, *The Book of Chuang Tzu*.)

A woodcarving in Guan Gong Temple, Shenzhen, depicting the landscape and buildings of an old Chinese town.

obsessed with tasks, routines, successes—all the things that stand in the way of true success—and to lose contact with the simple life of union with Dao, which is at the root of their being.

During Zhuangzi's lifetime the Zhou dynasty was overwhelmed with wars and conflict. It finally fell to the brief rule of the Qin (Ch'in) dynasty in 221 B.C.E. In 206 B.C.E. yet another dynasty came into power: The Han Dynasty.

The Han dynasty, which would reign until 220 C.E., eventually adopted Confucianism as the basis of state government. At the beginning, though, the rulers followed Daoist principles. They tried to interfere as little as possible with the lives of the citizens in order to allow them to recover from the years of bloodshed and war. During that time a number of Daoist sages studied Laozi and Zhuangzi and wrote commentaries on their work.

LIU AN AND THE HUAINAN MASTERS

Liu An (d. 122 B.C.E.) was the grandson of the first emperor of the Han dynasty and was the prince of Huainan. He invited scholars and wise men from all over the empire to come to his court, and he made it a center of learning in the arts and sciences.

According to legend a group of eight wise men appeared at Liu An's court seeking to join the hundreds of scholars already at work there. The prince, perhaps feeling that he already had enough wise men, asked them to prove that they had something new to offer. They so dazzled

---

EARLY CHINESE DYNASTIES

Legendary Period (Prehistoric Era–16th century B.C.E.)
> Mythical sage-emperors, including Huangdi, the Yellow Emperor

Shang Dynasty (16th–11th centuries B.C.E.)
> Fine bronzes appear
> Recorded history begins
> Silk is used extensively

Zhou Dynasty (ca. 1028–480 B.C.E.)
> *Yijing (I Ching)* compiled
> Golden Age of Philosophy (771–476 B.C.E.)
> Confucius (ca. 551–479 B.C.E.)
> Laozi (sixth century B.C.E.)
> Daoist Zhuangzi (fourth century B.C.E.)
> Daoist *Daodejing* compiled

Warring States Period (480–221 B.C.E.)

Qin Dynasty (221–207 B.C.E.)
> Chinese script, weights, and measures standardized
> Great Wall begun (214 B.C.E.)

Western Han Dynasty (206 B.C.E.–9 C.E.)
> Beginnings of papermaking
> Emperor Wang Mang overthrows dynasty, 9–23 C.E.

him with their knowledge and skill that he begged them to let him become their apprentice.

The lectures and lessons of these eight wise men are recorded in a series of essays that became a Daoist classic text, the *Huainanzi,* or "Masters of Huainan." This book is a collection of 21 essays. It is not purely Daoist in philosophy, as it incorporates some Confucian methods of self-improvement. The *Huainanzi* is an important work in its own right, but it also helped preserve the text of Laozi's work and guarantee its influence as it quotes extensively from the *Daodejing.*

ALCHEMY AND THE ELIXIR OF LIFE

One of Liu An's interests was alchemy, an offshoot of Daoist medical arts. The alchemists experimented with all kinds of magical spells and common materials—animal, vegetable, and mineral—as they tried to find a way to turn those common materials into gold. The goal of alchemy was not to create wealth, but to produce a formula for a golden potion—the so-called elixir of life—that would ensure immortality and everlasting youth.

In China there had long been magicians or "wonder workers," people who offered charms and secret words to ward off evil spirits and summon up good ones. These magicians were attracted to Daoist writings because they felt that many of them hinted at magical wonders. The Zhuangzi did include references to "perfect men," or immortals, who could pass through water without getting wet and through fire without getting burned. Those passages captured the imagination of many early followers of Daoism.

THE PATH TO IMMORTALITY

Around the fourth century B.C.E. scholars assembled a book called *The Yellow Emperor's Classic of Internal Medicine,* named for Huangdi, the great ancestor of Daoist tradition. The book's first chapter discussed ways to achieve immortality and long life. Many people came to believe that there must be a practical way to become immortal. Alchemists set about trying to find the specific formula for immortality. No alchemist ever found it, but emperors and kings never stopped desiring it and the alchemists never stopped pursuing it.

The path to immortality was a long and complicated process. It was necessary to achieve total physical and spiritual harmony through meditation, diet, exercise, breath control, the use of herbs, and other special practices. All disease had to be eliminat-

FOOD TECHNOLOGY

Liu An's court may have included hundreds of scientists who worked as alchemists and by chance made discoveries that furthered both science and medicine. Among their discoveries was a way to convert soybeans into bean curd, or tofu. While this food product did not prove to be the elixir of life, it did provide a valuable form of vegetable protein for people in a land where there was never enough meat. It also made the killing of animals unnecessary, thus contributing to Daoist principles.

A Chinese meal made with tofu and vegetables.

ed from the body and all evil eliminated from the spirit. The final step was to swallow the alchemical "golden potion." Although the elixir of life was known to be supremely dangerous for the imperfectly prepared person, it was believed that it would not harm anyone who had achieved earthly perfection. Indeed, no one could become immortal without taking the potion.

CHEMICAL DISCOVERIES

While hunting for this magical elixir the Daoist sages discovered many anesthetics and medicines. By learning how metals combined through heat they developed gunpowder and invented fireworks. They created chemical dyes and pigments as well as the glazes that make Chinese porcelain so beautiful. The understanding they gained of practical chemistry far exceeded that of any other culture at that time.

Before the *Huainanzi* became well known in the empire, however, political turmoil caused Liu An's downfall. He disappeared and the masters scattered. Soon after, Confucianism became the official state system of thought and education throughout the empire.

CHAPTER 3

THE GROWTH AND SPREAD OF DAOISM

The history of Daoism is one of political ups and downs. Daoists either enjoyed considerable favor, or had almost none at all. More often than not they were out of favor or at least observed with disapproval by the more conservative bureaucratic Confucians.

In the *Daodejing* Laozi had formulated a philosophy of government. "Governing a large country is like frying a small fish," he wrote. "You spoil it with too much poking." He advised rulers to fix their minds on Dao and stop meddling; later Daoists, such as Zhuangzi, developed this attitude even further. On the whole Daoists were not so much against government as above it. They were supremely disinterested. They preferred fishing in a mountain stream to shuffling papers in the imperial court.

Throughout history Daoism flourished in times of weak government and political chaos. Strong emperors, unless they were very secure and tolerant, tended to take a dim view of an

A Daoist temple on a wooded hillside in the Philippines. Daoism grew out of the natural environment, linking into the cycles of nature and the need to live in harmony with the earth.

Teacher and students practising martial arts in the United States. Daoists had a reputation for rebelliousness. They saw no conflict between their philosophy and fighting— there was almost always a war being waged in China, either internally or against invaders. War was a way of life recognized in the *Daodejing*. Laozi said, "In war, those who regard it as lamentable but necessary will win." Daoists studied swordplay and martial arts as part of their devotional practice. They elevated defense to a high art. Some of China's greatest military strategists were Daoists.

organization that preached anarchy—the concept that the best government was no government at all. Given a choice between the hardworking, rule-following Confucians or the Daoists with their minds turned toward nature and finding the Dao, the emperors usually chose Confucians. There were Daoists in most imperial courts, but they were engaged in alchemy, not government.

Emperors often regarded the Daoists, with their lack of respect for orderly government, as impudent and perhaps dangerous. From time to time a Daoist group would become powerful enough to seem a threat. Then Daoism was suppressed, usually brutally. Suppression in imperial China often meant that Daoist leaders were executed. Being a Daoist was risky. Even in the best of times political favor was unlikely to last. Daoism survived as a largely underground movement, attracting the disappointed, the unsuccessful, and those without privileges or legal rights. Yet survive it did, because it tapped into something deep in the Chinese consciousness.

> ### Journey of a Thousand Miles
>
> The *Daodejing* is the core text of Daoism, written somewhere between 400 and 300 B.C.E. It is a guide to living or even to ruling, and contains great wisdom about how to live. For example in this section the idea of being grounded, of knowing where you are and who you are before setting off on any adventure, is expressed in the line about how a journey of a thousand miles starts from beneath your feet.
>
> *Prevent trouble before it arises.*
> *Put things in order before they exist.*
> *The giant pine tree grows from*
> *a tiny sprout.*
> *The journey of a thousand miles starts*
> *from beneath your feet.*
>
> (In Stephen Mitchell, *Tao Te Ching: A New English Version*.)

THE SEEDS OF DAOISM

Laozi, Zhuangzi, and the other early Daoist sages meant their writings as practical guides for living. They were not thinking about starting a religion as Buddha did, nor were they consciously working to reform an existing religion as Jesus did. These early Daoist sages drew their ideas at least in part from ancient Chinese religious traditions, but their aim was to record their philosophy, their thoughts on society and government and the human condition. Their ideas are known as *Dao jia*—"Daoist thought," or the philosophy of Daoism.

Daoism's early followers were mostly people who searched individually for Dao. Some became deeply immersed in the alchemical or the governmental aspects of Dao. These followers attached themselves to imperial courts, where they amazed or advised emperors. Others withdrew from society altogether and became hermits, communing with nature deep in the mountains. Early Daoists in general had little interest in forming an organized religion. By the time of the Eastern Han dynasty (25–220 C.E.), however, some of the Daoist sages were attracting a following. The Confucian-based government no longer seemed to be working. People who were looking for an alternative found it in the *Daodejing*.

DAOISM BECOMES A RELIGION

The first Buddhist missionaries had come to China from India in the first century C.E. As time went on they steadily became more active in winning converts. Buddhism was an attractive religion, and by the second century C.E. it was spreading rapidly. It was not Chinese, however. Although many people were dissatisfied with ethical, rule-oriented Confucianism, they clung to the Chinese folk religions. Like Buddhism, those ancient religions featured many gods along with ghosts, demons, and evil spirits.

Beginning in the second century Daoism in the northern provinces of China began to change in the hands of a man named Zhang Daoling (Chang Tao Ling), whose family had been Daoists and alchemists for generations. Zhang saw the growing influence of Buddhism. He understood that Buddhism was spreading in China, in part because it had many gods and goddesses and magical rituals similar to those of the ancient Chinese folk religions. Bud-

Dao Jiao

Under Zhang Daoling Daoism acquired a new set of characteristics, including the belief in many gods and goddesses, the practice of casting magical spells, and the institution of a set of rituals to be followed. In some ways this new religion was like Buddhism. Its character, however, was decidedly Chinese. For his new faith Zhang established a religious organization with a hierarchy of spiritual leaders. He drew together many elements into a coherent whole. Because of this he is credited with being the founder of *Dao jiao*, religious Daoism.

Scroll painting of the immortal Zhang Daoling, the founder of religious Daoism, riding a tiger. The immortals had great spiritual and physical powers and would appear from time to time to help people in need.

dhism was not as abstract, or theoretical, as Daoism was, and it was not based mainly on a code of ethics as was Confucianism. It offered the spiritual comfort of ritual and close contact with gods who could influence daily life.

It is said that in the year 142 the spirit of Laozi, now a god in heaven, appeared to Zhang Daoling. The immortal spirit of Laozi gave Zhang Daoling the authority to establish a religion, a specific system of beliefs and worship, that would replace the many folk religions with one based on Daoist principles.

Zhang Daoling called his movement Tian Shi, or "Way of the Celestial Masters." He himself became the first celestial master, taking his authority from Taishang Laojun, which means "Divine Lord Lao"—that is, Laozi. Under Zhang Daoling, the *Daodejing* came to be viewed as a divinely revealed book because it was the work of the deified Laozi.

Zhang Daoling became known as a healer and exorcist. He connected sickness with sin, either one's own sin or the sin of an ancestor. He devised rituals to cleanse people of their sins and heal them. Those seeking healing would write their sins on a piece of paper and wade into a river, holding the paper above their heads, until their sins were washed away. Thus Zhang offered not only physical cures, but also spiritual and psychological healing. Through the Daoism of Zhang Daoling an ordinary person, as opposed to a teacher or sage, might hope for salvation.

Zhang traveled the countryside casting out demons and curing diseases. As an alchemist he had knowledge and skill that few people possessed. He achieved some miraculous cures, drawing many converts to the new faith.

THE RISE OF DAOCRACY

Other Daoist masters had gathered followers but Zhang drew his into an organization divided into 24 units, or parishes, each centered on a place of worship called an oratory. The oratory was overseen by a priest called a libationer, to whom Zhang delegated ritual powers. When a follower brought a problem or a wish to the libationer, it was the libationer's duty to determine which of the many Daoist gods and spirits should be petitioned to deal with it and to send it on the appropriate way. There were three Daoist heavens, each one higher than the last and each with many sections, not unlike the government of a large Chinese city of the time. Indeed the Daoist heavens are often referred to as the "heavenly bureaucracy."

Once a petition reached the proper heavenly department the official gods of that precinct would hear it and rule on its merit. Then if they chose they could summon the necessary heavenly forces against the demon causing the trouble.

GROWTH OF POLITICAL POWER

Members of the community also met to celebrate feasts in which the sharing of food was a communion, or spiritual union, with Dao. In addition to regularly scheduled feast times community members met to celebrate religious occasions and for other group activities. Their community activities helped to keep them together as a group and to keep the Daocracy functioning.

To support the system the Daoist organization taxed each household five pecks (an outdated measurement equivalent to 10 gallons in volume) of rice. Because of this tax Zhang's movement was mocked by the Confucians as the Way of the Five Pecks of Rice (instead of Way of the Celestial Masters). However the movement was strong both religiously and politically. Its strength and integrity may even have contributed to the Han dynasty's ultimate downfall.

When the Han dynasty failed, the well-organized Way of the Celestial Masters gained substantial political power. Zhang Lu was able to set up a small, independent, religion-centered state in what is now Shaanxi Province in eastern China. Under his rule inns were constructed that would be free for travelers, alcoholic beverages were banned, new roads were built, and food banks were established to feed the poor. Zhang Lu established a system of justice that featured rehabilitation of criminals through faith and kindness. On the whole life in the Daocracy was substantially better than life in much of imperial China.

DEMON-SLAYING SWORD

Zhang Daoling is said to have received a sword and a seal from heaven. With these, and with magic charms he had received from Laozi, he was able to capture and slay demons. At the end of his earthly life Zhang Daoling became immortal and the sword passed to his descendants for their use in protecting the people from evil. His son Zhang Heng and then his grandson Zhang Lu took over the leadership of the Celestial Masters, establishing a line of spiritual leaders who are often referred to as the popes of Daoism.

A late-18th-century scroll painting from a Daoist temple in southern China. This banner, depicting exorcist and protector deities, is specifically brought out at the festival of Hungry Ghosts to ward off evil. Zhang Daoling, raising his devil-chasing sword, is on the lower left side of the banner.

The insights and wisdom gained were recorded in one of the classics of Daoism, the *Taipingjing*—the *Classic of Great Peace*—and its teachings have helped shape Daoism to this day.

DAOISM IN THE WEI DYANSTY

In spite of the turmoil in China as the Han dynasty came apart, the Daocracy of the Zhang family lasted 30 years. Then in 215 Zhang Lu agreed to submit to the authority of a Han general, Cao Cao (Ts'ao Ts'ao), whose forces had subdued the surrounding territory. Only six years later China split into three states: Wei, Shu, and Wu. Cao Cao became the founder of the Wei dynasty, which lay in the north. He formally recognized the sect of the Celestial Masters. They in turn agreed to support the government as long as it was run on Daoist principles. The arrangement proved to be mutually beneficial and the Way of the Celestial Masters continued to win followers in the courts of the Wei rulers throughout the third century.

THE WAY OF GREAT PEACE

One of the central themes of the *Daodejing* is government. Laozi had described a society in which all people worked together in harmony and contentment, with little governmental interference. The *Zhuangzi* related this governmental ideal to the legendary rule of the Yellow Emperor and to other great sage-emperors thousands of years earlier. Confucian texts too glorified this ancient time called the *Taiping*, or "Great Peace."

A PERFECT SOCIETY

These texts inspired the dream of a utopia, a perfect society. In the second century the dream became a popular movement in the eastern provinces under the leadership of a Daoist named Zhang Jue (Chang Chueh).

Zhang Jue foretold 10 years of political disasters and natural catastrophes. He promised, however, to protect those who followed him and repented of their sins. The Han rulers were weak and corrupt and people could easily imagine the troubles Zhang

Jue predicted. His vision of a serene and peaceful government appealed to them. His movement became immensely popular. Zhang Jue hoped to create a society in which the search for Dao would be the supreme goal. His society would center on the pursuit of Dao and everyone would live according to Daoist principles. The *Daodejing* of Laozi would serve as a guidebook to the art of perfect government.

THE YELLOW HEAVEN

In 184 C.E. Zhang Jue announced that the "blue heaven" of the Han dynasty, which came from the east where blue-green was the symbolic color, was to be replaced by the "yellow heaven" of his perfect society. The Chinese character for *blue* also stood for *old,* a reference to the old and now corrupt eastern Han rule.

Yellow was the color of the central districts of China from which Zhang Jue came. His followers, by now more than 200,000 strong, wore yellow turbans. They worshipped Huang Lao—a deity whose name was a combination of the names of Huangdi (the Yellow Emperor) and Laozi.

Under the slogan "The Blue Heaven has died and the Yellow Heaven is coming to Power," the Yellow Turbans rose in revolt against the government. Mobs burned towns and ransacked the homes of the ruling classes. Eventually the superior army of the Han dynasty put down the rebellion and the survivors scattered. Some fled to the north, where they joined a Daoist movement that had already begun there. The Yellow Turban revolt of 184 was the first of many similar rebellions with Daoist elements that occurred throughout history, often in times of foreign occupation.

DAOISM IN THE SOUTH

Early in the fourth century C.E. northern China was repeatedly invaded by various nomadic tribes that came sweeping in on horseback from Manchuria, Mongolia, Tibet, and other lands farther to the north. Many of the celestial masters migrated to the south.

A Daoist priest in traditional robes in the courtyard of a Daoist temple on Hua Shan sacred mountain in Shaanxi Province. Hua Shan is known as the mountain of the west and is one of the five sacred Daoist mountains of China.

CONVERSIONS TO DAOISM

Arriving in the southeast from the war-torn north, the celestial masters began an active campaign to win people away from the old folk religions and over to Daoism. They succeeded in attracting converts from many of the aristocratic families in the region and their numbers grew steadily. However their form of Daoism was about to change once again with the emergence of the Highest Purity movement, Yang Xi's transformed and reshaped form of Daoism.

Rice growing in paddy fields among the karst (limestone) mountains near Yangshuo, Guilin, southern China. Daoists sought union with the Dao that could be felt in the natural harmony and balance of the land.

Other Daoists had been there before them. The most influential was Ge Hong (Ko Hung, 283–343 C.E.), a student of Daoist philosophy and alchemy. He had an active career in government and the military and also managed to write widely on many topics. His book *Baopuzi,* or *He Who Holds to Simplicity,* attempted to draw together Confucian ethics and Daoist beliefs. The Baopuzi is one of the earliest and most complete descriptions of the alchemists' search for the elixir of life. It explained Daoist belief in immortality and developed the idea of working toward "spiritual alchemy," or perfection without alchemical formulas. Finally, it established a merit system for doing good works as a necessary part of achieving immortal life.

A charismatic leader, Ge Hong helped to prepare the way for the new religion to take hold.

THE HIGHEST PURITY SECT

Beginning in 364 a Daoist named Yang Xi (Yang Hsi), an official in the imperial court, had a series of visions. In those visions, which lasted until 370, he saw a group of immortals, people who had achieved spiritual and physical perfection and had been taken up into the Highest Purity Heaven of the Daoists. They revealed to him a whole new body of scripture and much practical information. The immortals are said to have told Yang Xi that the period in which he was living, marked by war, disease, and the worship of false gods, would end in fire and flood and would be replaced by a rule of Dao.

THE MAO SHAN SCHOOL

Yang Xi saw that to bring about the rule of Dao in the south, the northern Way of the Celestial Masters would have to adapt to southern ways. He set about making the necessary reforms. Yang Xi's genius enabled him to bring together elements of Buddhism and local religions along with traditional Daoist beliefs. He transformed and reshaped many elements of Daoism.

Yang Xi's transformations came to be called both the Highest Purity movement and the Mao Shan school, named for Mount

Mao where it was founded. Mao Shan rises south of the Yangtze River near Shanghai and Nanjing.

The Highest Purity Daoists greatly enriched the practices and rituals of the Way of the Celestial Masters and strengthened Daoism. The Highest Purity Daoists emphasized the use of meditation and withdrawal from the world to allow a return to the "pure" principles of Daoism. This movement also produced a number of exceptional thinkers, one of whom was Dao Hongjing (Tao Hung Ching, 456–536), who became the foremost Daoist master of his time.

Dao Hongjing emphasized the importance of *wuwei*, the emptying of the mind of all thought so that Dao might enter.

RITUALS AND LITURGIES

Dao Hongjing was a close friend of Emperor Wu Di of the Liang dynasty (502–56). The Wu emperor had been a Daoist in his youth but he later became a fervent Buddhist. In 504 the emperor banned all Daoist groups. However, he honored his close friendship with Dao Hongjing and he and his followers were allowed to continue their work, thus preserving the community of Daoists at Mao Shan. Dao Hongjing's influence is still felt among Mao Shan Daoists. From his teachings his disciple Wang Yuanji (Wang Yuan Chi) created liturgies and rituals of great beauty and appeal that are still being used and that continue to attract people to Daoism.

Other Daoist movements developed in the south. Their leaders, like those of the Highest Purity movement, tried to adapt Daoism into a dynamic, popular religion. Among all of the groups, however, the Highest Purity Daoists founded by Yang Xi remained the most prominent form of Daoism in the south.

DAOISM IN THE NORTH

In the north, meanwhile, the Way of the Celestial Masters was undergoing a rebirth. In 415 Kou Qianzhi (K'ou Ch'ien-chih) had a visitation from Divine Lord Lao (Laozi) in which Lao named him Celestial Master and instructed him to reform Daoism. Kou set out to bring the Way of the Celestial Masters into line with the writings of Laozi. He denounced certain practices, such as the tax

THE HUNDRED-CHARACTER TABLET OF LU YAN

This inscription on meditation by Lu Yan, or Lu Dongbin, one of the founders of Daoism, stresses the importance of blocking out thoughts of wordly things as these have no benefit. Then, craving and irritation with everyday situations will disappear and one will sense peace and quiet.

Nurturing energy, forget words and guard it.
Conquer the mind, do non-doing.
In activity and quietude, know the source progenitor.
There is no thing; whom else do you seek?
Real constancy should respond to people;
In responding to people, it is essential not to get confused.
When you don't get confused, your nature is naturally stable;
  when your nature is stable, energy naturally returns.
When energy returns, elixir spontaneously crystallizes, in the pot
  pairing water and fire.
Yin and yang arise, alternating over and over again, everywhere
  producing the sound of thunder.
White clouds assemble on the summit,
  sweet dew bathes the polar mountain.
Having drunk the wine of longevity,
  you wander free; who can know you?
You sit and listen to the stringless tune,
You clearly understand the mechanism of creation.
The whole of these twenty verses
Is a ladder straight to heaven.

(In Thomas Cleary, *Vitality, Energy, Spirit: A Taoist Sourcebook.*)

A statue of the Jade Emperor, the ruling deity of heaven, that has been specially erected in Hong Kong for festivities to mark the Hungry Ghost Festival. The Song emperor Zhen Zong (Chen Tsung, 998–1020), a Daoist, added to the hosts of heaven by declaring additional gods and immortals and giving them ranks in the heavenly hierarchy. The god known as the Jade Emperor had the most powerful position, ruling as he did over the gods of earth and water and such immortals as Laozi and the Yellow Emperor. These heavenly folk waged a continual battle against the evil spirits and demons in the Ten Courts of the Underworld.

of five pecks of rice, as corrupt and corrupting. "What have such matters to do with the pure Dao?" he cried angrily.

Kou's proposed reforms won the attention—and the favor—of the Wei emperor Tai Wu Di, who gave him power over all religious practices of the state and proclaimed Daoism the official religion of the empire. In return Kou gave the emperor a Daoist insignia, designating him the earthly representative of Divine Lord Lao on earth. Thus in the north and throughout China Daoism continued to have an influence on Chinese government and cultural life.

DAOISM UNDER THE TANG EMPERORS

In 618 a new dynasty came into power, finally bringing peace. Under the Tang emperors China was once again unified. The Tang dynasty would rule China until 907, almost 300 years. Their rule was marked by great achievements in poetry, sculpture, painting, and scholarship.

The official religion of the Tang state was Confucianism, but the founder of the dynasty was Li Yuan, who traced his ancestry back to Li Ehr, or Laozi himself. Under the leadership of Li Yuan and his descendants Daoism won increasing favor. Although it again did not become the official state religion, it had the government's respect.

The Mao Shan, or Highest Purity Daoists, were the dominant group of the time. The most famous Highest Purity Daoist of the Tang era was Sima Cheng-zhen (Ssuma Ch'eng-chen, 647–735). He became the spiritual master to emperors and his treatise on meditation became a classic.

DAOISM AND THE SONG DYNASTY

The fall of the Tang dynasty in 907 ushered in a period of warfare and political confu-

DAOIST LITERATURE BEYOND CHINA

Under the Tang the *Daodejing* slowly increased in importance as a sacred work, and every family in the empire was required to have a copy. Meditation, alchemy, and magic were popular. Laozi's birthday became a national holiday and the dynasty built Daoist temples and monasteries at Mount Mao and Mount Song. In particular they built a huge Academy of Daoism at the legendary site where Laozi wrote his *Daodejing* before going west. Louguantai is still a major center for Daoism today. Aided by the creation of this great Academy at Louguantai, Daoist literature spread throughout the empire and across the borders into Tibet and India.

sion that ended when the Song dynasty (960–1279) emerged. Under Song emperors Daoism again became the official state religion. The Song rulers officially recognized the claim of the leaders of Highest Purity Daoism that their lineage back to Zhang Daoling, the founder of religious Daoism, was unbroken.

CREATING A HARMONIOUS WHOLE

By this time Daoist masters had come to realize that there was no golden elixir of life. During the Mao Shan revelations the immortals who appeared to Yang Xi had given him formulas for elixirs that they said were their food and drink. They cautioned, however, that these elixirs would be deadly poisons to mortals. The search for alchemical gold was officially discouraged. While still teaching techniques of longevity and spiritual improvement, Daoist masters rejected the notion of a chemical elixir. Alchemy came to be understood as spiritual, a blend of the elements of body, mind, and spirit into a harmonious whole.

Immortality, though, remained a major concern of Daoism. Among the common people, a tradition was evolving concerning a class of heavenly beings known as immortals. For people who had practiced a folk religion before coming to Daoism the spirit world was more real than the emperor's court. The immortals were folk heroes, in some cases historically well-known people who were believed to have achieved physical as well as spiritual immortality, often through suffering. They would appear in ordinary society from time to time, do good works (or create mischief for evildoers), and then be assumed into heaven once again. The immortals came to occupy an important place, much like that of Christian saints.

DRAGON-TIGER MOUNTAIN

In the Song period temples and monasteries were established in every province. In 1015 the emperor granted the celestial masters a large area of land at Lung Hu Shan, or Dragon-Tiger Mountain in what is now Jiangxi (Kiangsi) Province in southeastern China. This was to be their stronghold until they were driven out by the

LATER CHINESE DYNASTIES

Eastern Han Dynasty (25–220)

Fine paper produced (105)

Silk Road developed for trade throughout Asia

Yellow Turban Rebellion (184)

Three Kingdoms Dynasty (221–265)

Shu, Wei, Wu kingdoms established

Rise of Buddhism

Increasing importance of Daoism

Jin Dynasty (265–589)

Increased influence of Buddhism

Invasions from the north (early fourth century)

Sui Dynasty (590–618)

China reunified (589)

Buddhism and Daoism favored

Canal system established

Confucian system of civil service examinations introduced

Tang Dynasty (618–906)

Great achievements in poetry, sculpture, painting

Rise of scholar-officials in government

Territorial expansion

Five Dynasties (907–960)

China divided into independent kingdoms

Non-Chinese control North China

First military use of gunpowder

Song Dynasty (960–1260)

China reunified

Great age of landscape painting

Neo-Confucianism dominates

Genghis Khan conquers North China (1167–1227)

Period of warfare with Mongols

Yuan Dynasty (1260–1368)

Mongol dynasty established by Kublai Khan

Growing contact with the West; visits of Marco Polo

Confucianism, Daoism discouraged

Ming Dynasty (1368–1644)

Mongols expelled

Civil service examinations and Confucianism reinstated

European traders and missionaries in China

Qing Dynasty (1644–1911)

Established by Manchus

European influence grows

Chinese power weakens

Dynastic rule ends

Chinese Communists in 1930. Under the Song emperors many Daoist works were collected, and an encyclopedia was compiled to preserve early Daoist writings.

Printing had become widespread in China, and in 1016 the emperor supported the printing of the Daoist canon, the *Dao-zang (Dao Ts'ang)*, the collected works that were the main resource of the Daoist religion. Daoism was now dominated by the two organizations that had stood the test of time—the Highest Purity movement and the Way of the Celestial Masters.

THE COMPLETE REALITY SECT

In 1126 a wave of Tartar invaders came down from the north, toppling the Song emperor. A Song prince escaped and set up a new government along Confucian lines. Confucianism, however, had changed. Influenced by Daoism Confucian thinkers began to consider for the first time the philosophical questions of being and other problems of human existence.

RETURN TO ANCIENT DAOISM

In the south of China, Daoism was repressed. In the occupied north, however, new Daoist groups sprang up. The strongest of these groups was the Complete Reality movement (Quanzhen), a revival movement founded by Wang Chongyang (Wang Zhe, 1113–70).

The Complete Reality movement was marked by a return to the naturalness and freedom that had characterized ancient Daoism. Its leaders recommended "clear serenity" for their followers. They traced their branch of thought back to Lu Yan, a Daoist of the Tang era (618–906) who became known as Ancestor Lu. A Confucian scholar, Lu Yan came to Daoism in middle age. According to belief he became immortal in body as well as spirit; he reappears in times of trouble to help those who call on his power. Lu Yan left behind a body of writing that integrated Buddhist and Confucian thought with philosophical, religious, and alchemical Daoism. Later Complete Reality Daoists built increasingly on this blending of traditions.

A Mongolian dressed as a traditional 13th-century warrior. In 1215 Genghis Khan led a Mongol army campaign against the Jin dynasty in northern China and captured their capital, Yanjing (later known as Beijing). Genghis Khan was tolerant of Daoism and allowed the religion to be practised freely.

IN THE COURT OF GENGHIS KHAN

The Complete Reality Daoists attracted the attention of the Mongol rulers of the north. The famous Mongol conqueror Genghis Khan invited Wang's successor, Qiu Chuji (Ch'iu Chang Chun, 1148–1227), to come to his court and preach. Genghis Khan asked Qiu for the elixir of life but the master would offer only Daoist principles of health and serenity. Nevertheless Genghis Khan looked kindly on the Daoists, and through Qiu's efforts Daoists were permitted to continue to worship freely.

REVERSALS UNDER THE YUAN DYNASTY

Genghis Khan's grandson, Kublai Khan, was less benevolent than his grandfather. Kublai Khan made Buddhism the official religion of his Yuan dynasty, which ruled China from 1279 to 1368, and he commanded that almost all Daoist books be seized and burned. He allowed only the *Daodejing* and Daoist books on medicine, pharmacy, and science to be preserved.

As a result of Kublai Khan's decree Daoist literature dating back more than 10 centuries was destroyed. Daoism, however, could not be wiped out; instead it went underground. All across China Daoism's followers saved what literature they could, and what they could not save they kept alive in the oral tradition. Revolts in South China and Mongolia weakened the rule of Kublai Khan. In 1368 a leader named Zhu Yuanzhang drove the Mongols out of Peking (now Beijing) and seized power, establishing the Ming dynasty (1368–1644). By 1382 the last of the Mongol invaders were driven out of China and peace returned.

DAOISM UNDER THE MINGS

Under Ming rule the native culture of the Chinese people was restored. The government enacted a new code of law free of all Mongol elements and practices. Walls, temples, shrines, highways, and gardens were rebuilt. At the direction of the Ming emperor scholars began compiling a collection of the best of Chinese literature and thought. Although the first emperor was Buddhist, he was tolerant of all of China's religions. He promoted Confucianism for the state but encouraged other faiths as well. The result was a renewed interest in Daoism and Buddhism among the common people and a surge in religious learning among scholars. In 1444 the Daoist canon was published in a form that it retains to this day. It was a monumental achievement of scholarship and printing.

THE QING DYNASTY

In 1644, after many years of warfare, an army from Manchuria, northeast of China, swept into Beijing and conquered it. These peoples, the Manchus, established the Qing (Ching) dynasty (1644–1911), which would be the last dynasty of China.

Although they spoke a different language and came from a different background, the Manchus left the customs of the Ming government fairly intact. They made few major changes in Chinese society or in the economy and they took a lenient attitude toward religion. One of the changes they did make was to require Chinese men to adopt Manchu clothes and to wear their hair long in a pigtail, or braid, as a sign of submission. Daoist priests, however, were exempt from these requirements.

As early as the Tang period attempts were made to fuse Daoism, Confucianism, and Chinese Buddhism into one religion, all of which met with varying success. One of those movements was the Great Success movement, or Dacheng Jiao (Ta Ch'eng Chiao). Begun by Lin Zhaoen (Lin Chao-en, 1517–98) during the Ming period, it was heavily Confucian but incorporated aspects of all three faiths. Generally Buddhists and Confucians kept to their own ways, but many Daoists adopted the fusion viewpoint. By the time of the Qing dynasty as many as 10,000 followers would meet to read from the *Da Xue (Ta Hsueh)*, or *Great Learning*, which merged the three great traditions of China.

Yet Daoism persisted as a separate entity. In many cases Daoist priests preached the moral beliefs of the three religions to the masses while passing on Daoist techniques of inner development to people secretly initiated into the Daoist way. It would take an outside influence to clarify the situation.

By the 16th century Daoist experimentation with minerals, plants, and animals—part of the search for good health and the elixir of life (the search for immortality) —had produced 52 chapters on medicinal drugs, together known as the *Great Pharmacopoeia.* This volume demonstrated Daoism's effect on science and medicine. Throughout the Qing period (1644–1911) individual Daoist masters like Liu Yiming (ca. 1737–1826) continued to study ancient works and to write commentaries on them. One of his most famous treatises explained the *Yijng (I Ching),* one of the ancient Chinese Five Classics and a book of prophecy and wisdom that dates to the century before Confucius. Translated into English by a contemporary scholar in the early 19th century, it was one of the first volumes to make Chinese thought and philosophy accessible to the West.

Shelves stocked with herbal remedies in a shop selling traditional Chinese medicine. Shops such as this can now be found in virtually every city in the world.

THE TAIPING REBELLION

Christian missionaries had been in China since late in the 16th century. By the mid-19th century the increase in trade between China and Europe and Britain encouraged more Christian missionaries to establish themselves in China, and Christianity spread among the common people. In keeping with the Chinese tradition of accepting more than one truth, Christian ideals became mixed with the existing religions of China.

A young man named Hong Xiuchuan (Hung Hsiueh Chuan), who had received Confucian training but repeatedly failed his civil service examination, stated that he was the younger brother of Jesus, appointed by God to wipe out the Manchu dynasty. Echoing Zhang Jue's words 1,700 years earlier, Hong called his movement *Taiping*, or "Great Peace," and like Zhang Jue he promised to bring a new heaven to earth with himself as Messiah.

The Taiping rebellion drew its followers from among the Chinese peasants and was a mixture of Christianity, Chinese folk religion and Confucianism. From 1850 to 1864 Hong waged war on the Chinese establishment, capturing city after city until he controlled most of southern China. The rebellion was finally put down by a combination of government troops and Western forces. In their time of power, the Taiping rebels had often singled out Daoist temples for destruction. It was the first sign that difficult times were coming for the Daoists of China, seen as they were as symbols of China's past and to many as part of its "superstitious" past. Western ideas presented Daoism as a primitive religion ill suited to the modern age.

DAOISM IN THE MODERN AGE

Eventually the increasing presence of Westerners led to antiforeign sentiment among the native Chinese. An uprising in 1900 against all Westerners was put down by an international force of European, American, and Japanese troops. The Manchu government, already weakened, found itself under still greater foreign influence. In 1911 it fell to yet another rebellion, and the long rule of the great Chinese dynasties was at an end.

The establishment of the Chinese Republic in 1912 was followed by decades of conflict—both civil war and war with Japan. Eventually this became a struggle between Communist and Nationalist forces within China. The two sides joined briefly to fight the Japanese in World War II (1939–45), but after the war the internal struggle began again. In 1949 China fell to commu-

A portrait of Mao Zedong hangs above one of the entrances to the Forbidden City in Tiananmen Square, Beijing. In 1949, Mao Zedong led the Communist rebels to victory against the nationalist forces.

nism and all religion was outlawed. The Nationalist Chinese fled to Taiwan, an island off the coast of mainland China, where they set up a competing government. One of the refugees was the 63rd celestial master of the Daoist faith, the spiritual descendant of Zhang Daoling, who had established a religion based on Daoist principles in 142. At the great Daoist centers on the mainland—places like Dragon-Tiger Mountain, where the celestial masters had established their center, and Mount Mao, where the Highest Purity sect was founded—the practice of Daoism was officially forbidden but never quite stamped out. As it had so many times before, it lived on in the minds and hearts of the Chinese people.

CHAPTER 4

THE SCRIPTURES AND BELIEFS OF DAOISM

The earliest writings on Daoism can be traced to the fourth century B.C.E. As Daoist sects arose, such as the Way of the Celestial Masters and the Highest Purity movement, their followers worked tirelessly to record their beliefs, liturgy, and rituals. Writings on Daoist themes continued steadily. The approach of each sect differed greatly in detail and emphasis. Some sects, such as the Highest Purity Daoists of Mao Shan, stressed the importance of meditation as a means of finding Dao, while others concentrated on recording rituals and spells, alchemical formulas, and ways to gain immortality. However taken as a whole the sects had a profound effect on Chinese thought. They extended Daoist philosophy beyond the imperial courts to workers and peasants, and they developed a complex system of beliefs that was distinct from both Chinese folk religions and other Chinese religious traditions.

The most popular figures in Chinese folklore are the Eight Immortals, a company of comic and tragic figures who help the poor and punish the wicked. This Daoist temple roof is decorated with carvings of these characters.

In the year 471 C.E. Daoist monks brought together the first *Dao-zang*, or Daoist canon. It drew from all of the main traditions of Daoism. The various sects recognized a common basis in the *Daodejing*, which, according to legend, stemmed from the 5,000-character manuscript Laozi left behind as he was leaving Luoyang

The Daoist canon was written using brush and ink on handmade paper similar to this modern brush and scrolls. The writing of the *Daozang,* the first Daoist canon, is full of cryptic symbols and references whose meanings have been lost over time. However the modern *Daozang* is still the primary source of Daoist thought. It contains the philosophy that lies at the root of Daoist belief, as well as the tales and parables, rituals and practices that have transmitted the Daoist religion down through the centuries.

and the Zhou court. Its interpretation by later masters gave rise to much of the rest of the canon, and it is the primary source for Daoist studies on the meaning of life. Since the second century C.E. Daoists have considered the *Daodejing* to be divinely revealed scripture.

The first Daoist canon contained 1,200 scrolls. Besides including the interpretations of the *Daodejing*, the canon included writings on alchemy and immortality, the lives of immortals and heroes, and good works and longevity. It had philosophical essays and folktales, magic words and meditation, ritual and liturgy, and many other aspects of Daoist thought.

In 748 the Tang emperor Tang Xuan-cong, who traced his ancestry to Laozi, sent scholars all over China to collect Daoist works. Not wishing to disappoint the emperor, the scholars reputedly returned with 7,300 scrolls. These scrolls became the second Daoist canon.

In about 1016, with printing established in China, the canon was revised under the direction of the Song dynasty. Some of the works collected under the Tangs were cast out, so the third canon contained only 4,565 scrolls.

A final version was produced in 1444 during the Ming dynasty (1368–1644). This work of 5,318 scrolls is the largest body of scripture in the world.

DAO AS THE ULTIMATE REALITY

The *Daodejing* begins with a question: What is Dao? The writer answers:

> The Dao that can be told is not the eternal Dao.
> The name that can be named is not the eternal Name.
> (In Stephen Mitchell, *Tao Te Ching: A New English Version*.)

According to the writer Dao is deeper than the deepest mystery the mind can imagine. It cannot be explained because it is too vast for human comprehension. Before anything existed there was Dao. When nothing exists any longer Dao will still be.

No one can fully explain Dao because the limited human mind does not have the capacity to understand it.

Dao cannot be seen, touched, or otherwise experienced with the senses, but it is expressed by the natural forces of the universe. Like the universe it is without beginning and without end. Zhuangzi, one of the great early Daoist masters, explains, "There is nowhere where it is not." However at the same time Dao is invisible and mysterious: what can be seen, heard, or felt is not truly Dao, which is above all things. The *Zhuangzi* says:

> *Dao has reality and evidence but no action and form.*
> *It may be transmitted, yet not possessed.*
> *It existed before Heaven and Earth and lasts forever . . .*
> (In Ch'u Chai and Wineberg Chai, *The Story of Chinese Philosophy*.)

THE ULTIMATE FORCE

Daoists believe the vast, formless Dao existed before anything else. From it came the origin of being, or One. From this One came the balance of opposing forces, yin and yang, which are opposite but inseparable. Yin and yang are expressed in the three forces of the universe: heaven, earth, and humanity. From these three come everything else. Thus Dao is the ultimate force or the reality behind everything.

Daoists accept that they can never fully understand Dao. What they focus on is finding a way to get into harmony with this ultimate force—to "go with the flow" of Dao and the universe.

NOT-BEING

The Dao from which all being comes is called the Great Void—an emptiness or "not-being." The Daoist seeks union with this emptiness, which is seen as a higher state than consciousness or thought. Daoists cultivate *wuwei*, which is often described as non-doing. This has sometimes been interpreted as an invitation to withdraw from society but it is actually a kind of higher action, one in harmony with the natural order.

TRANSLATING FROM THE CHINESE

The Chinese language has no tenses, no singulars and plurals, no articles, and makes no gender distinctions. A given character may be used as a noun or as a verb, or even both in the same sentence, and Chinese words have many shades of meaning. Readers of Chinese understand all of these meanings simultaneously. Translators can only try to capture the general idea of the original. Many translators feel that a free—that is, inexact—translation of Chinese is often closer to the intent of the original than a literal, or exact translation. Here for comparison are several translations of the first lines of Chapter 4 of the *Daodejing*.

All of these translations say the same thing, but not in the same way. All are "right"—that is, all are faithful to the general idea of the lines—yet all are different. The variations suggest why people have been reading and discussing the *Daodejing* for centuries and why many people say that there is no translation as good as reading it in the original Chinese.

The Way is like an empty vessel
That yet may be drawn from
Without ever needing to be filled.
It is bottomless; the very progenitor of all things in the world.
—Arthur Waley

The Way is a void
Used but never filled
An abyss it is Like an ancestor
From which all things come.
—R. B. Blakney

The Dao is empty (like a bowl)
It is used, though perhaps never full
It is fathomless, possibly the progenitor of all things.
—from deBary, *Sources of Chinese Tradition*

The Dao seems to be very hollow and transparent and empty, but when you use it, it's inexhaustible. It is very deep and mysterious. It's like the ancestor of all things.
—Al Huang

The Dao is like a well
used but never used up.
It is like the eternal void:
Filled with infinite possibilities.
—Stephen Mitchell

Wisdom and serenity come from conforming one's life to the natural laws of the universe. The notion of not-being is often associated with Daoist meditation, which requires an emptying of the mind so that the creative forces of Dao can flow in.

HARMONY AND BALANCE: YIN AND YANG

People cannot see Dao but they can experience it in the rhythmic cycles of nature: night and day, winter and summer, rain and sun, death and birth. These opposing forces of the natural world express the Chinese concept of yin and yang. The specific notion of yin and yang was not originally Daoist, but it chimed with what Laozi and the other early Daoist philosophers believed.

The concept of yin and yang is central to Daoist understanding. These two forces demonstrate Dao, and because Dao is in everything, yin and yang are a part of Dao. Yang is the heavenly force. It is the force of movement, of light, fire, warmth, and life. Yang literally means "the sunny side" of a hill. In Chinese, *sun* is *tai yang*, or "great yang."

Yin, the shady side of the hill, is yang's opposite, but it cannot be separated from yang. Just as there can be no shadow without sun, there can be no yin without yang. The two operate together, in the cycles that are a part of nature and of Dao.

THE RELATIVE UNIMPORTANCE OF ALL THINGS

The opposing forces represented by yin and yang are not permanently fixed. Daoists see all things as relative to one another. A cloudy day is yin—dark—when compared to a sunny one. However it is

A yin-yang symbol above the entrance to a Daoist temple in Jeonju, Korea.

BINDING THE UNIVERSE

The concept of yin and yang sums up all of the opposing forces in life. However as the Daoist sees it, these forces are not truly opposites. They complement each other, resolving their differences in the great circle that symbolizes the unity of Dao. The *Huainanzi* explains:

> *Dao can be concise, but stretched*
>   *quite long; dark, but shine brightly;*
> *weak, but become strong.*
> *It is the axle of the four seasons.*
> *It contains Yin and Yang,*
> *Binding together the universe . . .*
> *Long ago, in the very beginning,*
>   *the two emperors (Yin and Yang)*
> *having attained the Dao's authority,*
>   *were established in the center.*
> *Their spirits then spread far and wide,*
> *ruling the four directions.*
> *This is why the heavens move and the*
> *earth is stable.*
> *Turning and evolving without*
> *exhaustion . . .*
> *Like a potter's wheel, revolving round,*
>   *returning to the starting point.*

yang—bright—when compared to night. If you were to ask a Daoist whether something were "good or bad," a Daoist might respond, "Compared to what?"

To a Daoist good and bad, yes and no, are not very far apart, so it is possible to accept the troubles of life calmly. The way of nature is neither right nor wrong—it simply is. Daoists attempt to be like nature itself. In nature everything is constantly changing from yang to yin and back again. In life no one can tell how things may turn out. Indeed if one waits long enough what appears to be good fortune may turn out to be a disaster, and what seems to be bad luck may be good. Success and failure, wealth and poverty, fame and obscurity all have equal drawbacks. Thus all things are really the same in Dao.

DEVELOPING STILLNESS

In Daoism simply being, or getting along as nature does, comes ahead of achievement. Too much pride causes people to be brought low. Like water, Daoists take the low ground. Water in itself is soft and yielding but it melts the hardest things. It lies in the low places of the earth but it nourishes all life. This is the "valley spirit," which never dies.

To a Daoist creation is passive, yin, the "mysterious female" that gives birth to all. Daoists try to develop this stillness within themselves through meditation and devotional activities that bring calm and peace. In trying to be like nature they cultivate an appreciation for the natural world. Daoists are close to Dao in natural settings, on mountaintops, in tranquil woods, and in peaceful valleys.

PEOPLE AND THE WAY OF NATURE

In Daoism there is no rebirth into a heavenly kingdom after death as there is in Christianity. Nor is there reincarnation, or rebirth in another form as there is in Buddhism. The Daoist focuses on life here and now, life in this world. According to the 20th-century writer Lin Yutang, the Daoist is:

. . . one who starts out with this earthly life as all we can or need to bother about, wishes to live intently and happily as long as his life lasts, often has a sense of poignant sadness about this life and faces it cheerily, has a keen appreciation of the beautiful and the good in human life

The yin-yang symbol laid before the entrance of a Daoist temple. The darker section of the symbol represents yin which is heavy and dark and the power felt in the cold of winter. The lighter section is yang which is light and bright and the power felt in the heat of summer. These forces continually work together in a dynamic tension. The temple itself is set among trees, reflecting the closeness that Daoists feel for the natural world.

Daoism Reflects on Human Existence as Part of the Natural World:

Human life in the world is no more than that of a dayfly. This is true not only of ordinary people but also of the wizards and buddhas of all times as well. However, though a lifetime is limited, the spirit is unlimited. If we look on the universe from the point of view of our lifetime, our lifetimes are those of dayflies. But if we look on the universe from the point of view of our spirit, the universe too is like a dayfly.

—from *Sayings of Lu Yan*

Transformation in Life

A Daoist pursues immortality in the present life with the hope that by the time of death he or she will have been transformed. Ideally his or her real, immortal body will already be present within the shell of the mortal body that is visible to others. Daoists try to transform their bodies by nurturing the forces of yang, or life, within themselves.

whereever he finds them, and regards doing good as its own satisfactory reward.
(In Lin Yutang, *The Importance of Living.*)

Daoists hope to have a long earthly life and they try to do everything possible to see that they will have such a life. Living according to Daoist principles requires self-discipline, self-awareness, and self-control. Daoists resist the desires and excesses that threaten to rob them of life. They hope, through the practice of various life-enhancing activities such as exercise, meditation, and healthful diet, to live a very long time. They believe that by so doing they will become *xian*, able to achieve immortality in the present life. Daoists see human beings as a natural part of the universe. Therefore the life of a person who brings his or her life into complete harmony with the natural laws and cycles of the universe should continue to exist as long as heaven and earth exist.

Stories about Daoist sages describe how they became *xian*, or immortal. In these stories the sages died and were buried but later their coffins were opened to reveal not a body but a bamboo cane, a feather, or a sword. The Daoists understand these changes to mean that although the body appears to die, what has really died is the emblem to which the person has given his likeness. The person's true body has gone away and dwells in the paradise of the immortals.

THE THREE TREASURES

Daoism stresses the importance of preserving the "three treasures" of human life: vitality, energy, and spirit. These three elements are both inseparable and interdependent. One cannot exist without the other two. Vitality, or *jing (ching)*, is associated with creativity and with basic body functions, including procreation. Energy, or *qi (chi)*, the essence of life, is associated with movement and strength. Spirit, or *shen*, is associated with consciousness, intellect, and spirituality.

CULTIVATING *SHEN*

Daoists also cultivate aspects of *shen*, the center of all emotions, thoughts, and intentions. They understand that *shen* may be wasted through passions, distractions, excesses of *qi* or *jing*, and generally "going overboard." The *Daodejing* admonishes followers to be yielding and passive because "the gentlest thing in the world overcomes the hardest," and counsels against being ambitious or competitive:

> Fill your bowl to the brim and it will spill.
> Keep sharpening your knife and it will be blunt.
> Chase after money and security and your heart will never unclench.
> Care about people's approval and you will be their prisoner.
> Do your work, then step back. The only path to serenity.
>
> (In Stephen Mitchell, *Tao Te Ching: A New English Version.*)

This "stepping back" from the stresses of life brings a peace of mind that is a way of coming into greater harmony with Dao.

> When you realize where you come from,
> you naturally become tolerant,
> disinterested, amused,
> kindhearted as a grandmother,
> dignified as a king.
> Immersed in the wonder of the Dao,
> you can deal with whatever life brings you.
>
> (In Stephen Mitchell, *Tao Te Ching: A New English Version.*)

Worldly ambitions drain the energies. Turning away from desire and ambition is the way to become one with Dao.

These three elements must be kept in harmony and balance. *Qi* is especially important because of its influence on the other two; therefore Daoists have developed many practices aimed at controlling and preserving *qi*. One of these is Taijiquan, the system of movement aimed at helping people to control their *qi*, the energy flow within their bodies. Many of the movements of Taiji were developed from the movements of animals. In the grace and power of animals early Daoist masters saw natural *qi*. The stylized movements of Taiji help those who practice it to unite with that natural *qi* force. The names of the movements reveal their origins: swallow returning to nest, clutching eagle, crane standing on one leg, cat looking at the moon. The graceful, circular motions reflect the natural cycles that are Dao.

People practicing Taijiquan in a Beijing park. Throughout China, many thousands of people gather in the early morning to practice this system of movement that balances the flow of *qi* in the body.

Many lifelong Daoists are content to live with the understanding that they are a part of the universal reality that is Dao and that they will one day return to Dao when their earthly life ends. These Daoists strive to live according to Daoist philosophy, to maintain balance and calm. They work to bring their lives into harmony with Dao through meditation, diet, Taijiquan, and similar devotional practices.

Other Daoists, however, believe that in the words of Laozi, "Every being in the universe is an expression of Dao." They identify the different forces of nature and being with individual spirits or gods. Their beliefs are sometimes referred to as religious, or "popular" Daoism.

GODS OF ALL THINGS

There is a pantheon—a great glittering array of gods—for the person who follows religious Daoism; everything in the universe, both seen and unseen, is controlled by a god. There are gods of heaven and gods of earth, gods of longevity and gods of immortality, gods of medicine and health, and gods of mercy and conflict. There are gods for cities and gods for nature—rivers and streams, rain and wind, grass and trees. There is a god for every flower and a Queen of All Flowers. There are gods of the stars, Sire Thunder and Mother of Lightning, and powerful gods of the regions of earth—North, South, East, West, and Center.

There are gods for common, everyday things such as walls, roofs and ditches. One of the most popular of the gods is the kitchen god, sometimes known as the god of stoves, who oversees the home life of families and around whom one of the most common and popular domestic rituals is regularly celebrated.

MOUNTAINS, HEROES, AND ANCESTORS

In popular Daoist belief each mountain and river is ruled by a particular god. Some of these gods were once human, such as Zhang Daoling, the father of religious Daoism. His deified spirit now rules at Lung Hu Shan, Dragon-Tiger Mountain. The mountain gods are especially powerful and it is to the mountains that Daoists go when they want to be close to Dao. Achieving harmony with the natural world implies a closeness to nature, and the mountains are particularly sacred to Daoists.

Another category of celestials, or heavenly beings, is that of heroes and ancestors. Even before Daoism emerged as a religion the Chinese revered their ancestors as if they were gods. It is believed that ancestors can intercede with the gods to aid and protect their living descendants. Similarly Chinese heroes are also worshipped as gods. These heroic figures need not have been Daoists to be included in the Daoist pantheon—some Daoist gods were Confucians or Buddhists. They have become *shen*, or godlike, by doing great deeds for society, dying in battle, or displaying outstanding virtue and goodness.

THE THREE PURE ONES

At the top of the pantheon of gods, in the supreme, highest, prior heavens, reign the Three Pure Ones, the gods of heaven, earth, and human beings. The Three Pure Ones figure prominently in Daoist ritual. They are aspects of Dao that appear as "heavenly worthies" or celestial beings. The Three Pure Ones may be identified as Heavenly Worthy of Primordial Being, who represents the beginning of all existence; Heavenly Worthy of Numinous Treasure, who represents the mysterious and nameless Dao; and Heavenly Worthy of the Way and Its Power.

In some traditions the latter two Pure Ones may be personified as Laozi and either Huangdi, the Yellow Emperor, or Yu Huang, the Jade Emperor. However their specific identities are not important. Together they are the spirit and mystery of Dao and the highest goals of humanity.

THE JADE EMPEROR'S COURT

Beneath the prior heavens are the posterior heavens—a little lower yet still exalted. These heavens are ruled by the Jade Emperor and are crowded with lesser gods and immortals.

These heavens are organized much like the imperial court of ancient China. The Jade Emperor, Yu Huang, personally directs and manages all of the affairs of heaven and earth. It is important to note, however, that the Jade Emperor is not like the all-powerful one God of Judaism, Christianity, and Islam. He does not always get his way. The forces of yin and yang are at work even in the Daoist heaven, and heavenly life is a continuing struggle against the forces of evil that the Jade Emperor's own forces sometimes lose.

THE IMMORTALS

Among the Daoist gods is a group called the Eight Immortals. As immortals the eight can fly through the air, appear and disappear at will, and use their magic to help people in need. They are called on for such diverse matters as minor illnesses, evil spirits, desire for male offspring, money troubles, and hope for longevity.

Images of the Eight Immortals can be found almost everywhere in the world in which Chinese people work and live: in shrines or Daoist temples; painted on wall scrolls, fans, vases, and teapots; carved into wood, porcelain, and earthenware; or cast in bronze. Of these immortals some are more powerful than others and can act alone. Some can act only in cooperation with others. Each immortal has a symbol with which he or she is able to work magic.

Some of the Eight Immortals were historical figures, dating to around the time of the Tang dynasty or earlier. The most powerful of the eight, and also the most popular, is Lu Dongbin (Lu Tong Pin). The immortal Lu Dongbin is none other than Ancestor Lu, or Lu Yan, the forerunner of the Complete Reality Daoists and the author of the Hundred Character Tablet in the *Daozang*. A major figure in the history and philosophy of Daoism, he is associated in popular belief with medicine and eternal life. He also has power over evil spirits and he carries a sword with which he can tame demons if he is properly approached.

Zhungli Quan (Han Zongli), another of the Eight Immortals, was a Han dynasty general who converted to Daoism. Others, like Zhang Guolao and He Xiangu, were common folk who had

Painting of the immortal Zhungli Quan with his feathery fan. He is famous for longevity.

attracted the attention of the gods through suffering unjust treatment without complaint and giving to others unselfishly. Tested by the gods and found worthy, they became immortal.

PERSONAL GODS

In contrast to the gods whose origins lie entirely in natural phenomena, such as the gods of earth and water, are the many personal gods. These were once people who did great deeds during

THE *BA XIAN*
(EIGHT IMMORTALS OF THE DAOIST GODS)

Lu Dongbin, also known as **Lu Van,** is the historical figure on whose writings Quanzhen Daoism is based. Associated with medicine, he also has charms to tame evil spirits. His emblem is a sword.

Li Tieguai is associated with medicine. Bad-tempered and eccentric, he appears as a beggar. His symbol is the crutch and he fights for the poor and the weak.

Zhang Guolao, a great magician, carries a musical instrument. He is often consulted by families who desire male offspring.

Cao Goujiu, known as a stern judge, carries an imperial tablet of recommendation.

Han Xiangzi is a great poet and musician and the patron of musicians. His symbol is a jade flute.

Zhungli Quan (Han Zhongli), formerly a Han general, is associated with immortality. He carries a feathery fan that calms angry seas.

Lan Caihe, although touched by insanity, is favored by the gods. He may appear as either a man or a woman. He carries a magic flower basket.

He Xiangu is the only woman among the Eight Immortals. She carries a lotus flower.

their lifetimes and whose spirits therefore continue to exist. Over time they have been elevated to the status of gods by the declarations of religious leaders or emperors. They are often associated with particular areas of influence, and Daoists pray to them and request their help. Believers try to emulate the examples each of these personal gods set while living.

Such gods as She, god of land, and Hou Ji, god of agriculture, were legendary officials under the rule of the Yellow Emperor. Other gods, like the gods of rain and fire, can also be traced to legendary or historical figures.

THE DEMON WORLD

The gods of the Daoists are challenged by demons, or *kuei*, that plague the natural and human worlds. These demons may be natural forces such as typhoons, epidemics, and droughts. They may also be men or women who have died violent, meaningless deaths. Sometimes they are "orphan souls," people who have no families to remember them or who have been improperly buried and have no ancestor tablet to keep their memory alive.

These unhappy demons roam the world and cause sickness and other hardships. In their efforts to be remembered they use the forces of nature to draw attention to themselves. Daoists do not worship demons but they do believe they exist. Thus they try to bargain with them and placate them, often by asking a god or an immortal to intercede. The continuous struggle between gods and demons is part of the popular interpretation of yin and yang, the balance of opposing forces that is Dao.

A Daoist demon carved under a temple roof.

GENERAL KUAN YU

War heroes might also become personal gods. Kuan Yu, or Kuan Jung, was a famous general during the period of the Three Kingdoms in the early part of the third century C.E. Refusing to surrender in battle, he was captured and executed by the enemy. Each succeeding generation glorified his memory until one of the Tang emperors declared him a god. Because he was also known for keeping meticulous financial records he has become the patron of bookkeepers. A popular god in many temples, he is often depicted as standing nine feet tall with red cheeks, a magnificent black beard, and bushy eyebrows.

HEAVENLY EMPRESS

Another personal god is Sheng Mu, who was named Heavenly Empress during the Qing dynasty. The daughter of a fisherman, she helped the farmers, fishers, and their families in her village by casting out demons before she died at the age of 21. Now patron of fishers and farmers, she keeps with her two of the demons that she tamed. They act as messengers, bringing the needs of the people to her attention so that she can rush to their aid.

CHAPTER 5

RITUAL AND MEDITATION

Ritual, the formal acts that make up religious observance, has been an important feature of Daoist worship since the time of Zhang Daoling in the second century C.E. Today priests trained in ritual words and actions, meditation, and scripture lead intricate forms of worship and praise handed down through 64 generations of Celestial Masters. These rituals express the continuing renewal of the universe and remind people of the harmony of Dao, the balance of yin and yang, the interaction of heaven, earth, and humanity, and the constant struggle between order and chaos.

Daoist ritual is a feast for the senses. Colorful robes, banners, statues and paintings of gods and immortals, instrumental music and song, chanting, liturgy, dance, incense, candles, lamplight, and even firecrackers work together to create an experience rich with meaning for participants and observers.

Through their religious observances Daoists participate in keeping their world orderly and harmonious by celebrating the

A community festival makes its way through the streets of a town in Shaanxi Province. These colorful festivals can last several days and are part of major *jiao* or "offering" celebrations. The rituals enhance the fortune and welfare of the community by summoning gods to bless the people and the land.

ultimate reality of Dao. The rituals they practice promote the well-being of their families, their ancestors, and their community, and keep evil away.

THE *JIAO*

The basic Daoist ritual held to enhance the welfare of living people is the *jiao*. *Jiao* means "offering," so a *jiao* may be a simple ritual offering of wine and food at a family altar. However, it is often a far more elaborate celebration. A *jiao* may be performed as part of the regular observance of the Daoist calendar or for a special occasion such as the consecration of a new temple. A *jiao* of this type is not a single ritual but an entire ritual program, a series of individual rites conducted for different purposes such as summoning the gods, blessing the land, or redeeming lost souls. The ritual celebration may last for three days.

The priests, who often travel some distance to participate, select the rituals for the occasion. These vary with the length and purpose of the *jiao*. Any of these individual rituals may be conducted separately or in combination with others at other times during the year.

A major *jiao* celebration often includes a community festival. While the priests and other participants are performing rituals inside the temple the festival is going on outside. Only the priests, their attendants, and community leaders observe

Women in traditional costume watch a performance during a *jioa* celebration in Qingdoa, China.

the sacred rites. Other members of the community celebrate the *jiao* by attending the festival and enjoying the colorful pageantry when the priests come outside. Festivals feature such entertainment as theatrical presentations on Daoist themes and martial

arts demonstrations. Food stands are many and vendors sell religious items such as paper ghost money, which is burned in offerings. There is a brisk trade in firecrackers, which Daoists use to scare away any yin spirits that might be lurking nearby. Large papier-mâché figures, made for the occasion, serve as "guardians" of the festival and keep an eye on the proceedings. Both the festival in the streets and the ritual within the temple may go on for several days.

PREPARATIONS AND FIRST DAY

For three days before the *jiao* the priests live in the temple, preparing themselves. The night before the *jiao* begins the priests perform a purification ritual. Oil is heated to the boiling point in a wok, a bowl-shaped metal container. While the priests chant prayers and use a buffalo horn to summon the heavenly visitors, a "redhead," a priest wearing a red headdress, throws alcohol on the oil causing flames to shoot heavenward. Everything that will be used in the *jiao*—robes, scrolls, musical instruments, incense sticks, candles—is passed over the flames and made ready. The first day of the *jiao* begins with a procession of priests, acolytes, cantors, musicians, and the keeper of incense. The priests then call on the Three Pure Ones—the gods of heaven, earth, and humanity—to be present at the ritual. The high priest lights incense in each of the five directions of the universe and offers a general confession. In a second procession the priests offer incense to the gods.

Outside the temple the priests raise a long, rectangular, yellow banner to attract the gods' attention. The red inscription on the banner invites the gods to enter the temple and asks for their protection and help.

RITUALS AND OFFERINGS

The morning rituals are followed by a noon offering. Each priest performs a song and a dance, thus displaying his talents to the gods. Each priest then ceremoniously places a gift such as a flower, tea, a candle, or fruit on the altar. The noon offering is repeated every day of the *jiao*. Afternoon ceremonies may include the Division of the Lamps, a ritual that symbolizes the coming of light to the world. With the temple in total darkness, fire is brought into the temple and candles are lighted one at a time and placed before each of the Three Pure Ones, accompanied by the singing of hymns. The ritual represents these lines from the *Daodejing*:

> Tao gives birth to one,
> One gives birth to two,
> Two give birth to three,
> Three give birth to all things.
> (In Stephen Mitchell, *Tao Te Ching: A New English Version*.)

These lines also form the basis of the ritual for the Return to Unity, in which the separate lights representing "all things" are combined into one and finally embodied in the priest, who at that moment becomes one with the great void or Dao.

Throughout the day the priests perform other rituals. The consecration of a new temple, for example, may include rites to prevent fire and to enrich the soil and bring prosperity to the community. At day's end the priests invite the immortals to come from the sacred mountains and join the celebration. Then all of the participants chant prayers to suppress yin, the negative force of the universe, and encourage yang, the positive force. The priests say the prayers for the night and then seal the altar.

SECOND AND THIRD DAYS

The second day, like the first, is full of rituals, some calling on the gods to be present and others asking for the salvation of wandering souls or for the preservation of the community. Some rituals may be carried out at a distance from the temple, with the festival-goers joining the sacred procession.

On the third day the priests read from the scriptures and make memorial offerings. The afternoon includes a special offering to the Three Pure Ones. Part of the offering ritual includes the hanging of a large black banner from the ceiling of the temple. The banner represents the heavenly bridge that the divine guests will use to come to earth and then to return to their celestial home.

As music plays two of the celebrants sit, and all of the other participants kneel. The deities are invited once again, from the least to the most powerful. As the ritual proceeds three kneeling priests sing sacred verses, while the seated priests wave banners over the backs of the community representatives to drive away evil. A firecracker explodes and the music stops. This ritual is repeated six times. Then all of the participants stand and proceed to the altar, where incense and wine are offered to the Three Pure Ones. The banquet of the gods over, the altar is sealed once more and the *jiao* is ended.

THE UNIVERSAL SALVATION

Although it is not technically part of the *jiao*, or offering to the gods, a final ritual follows: the ritual of Universal Salvation. Its purpose is to comfort and appease the "homeless souls," the nameless dead who wander without having been given a proper burial. As the yellow banner outside the temple is taken down to be burned, the priests exit the temple chanting. There they find a huge banquet awaiting them, a banquet of every imaginable kind of food: cakes, bread, fruit—even canned goods. Sticks of incense perfume the table.

The priests bless the food. After another procession they display a writ, or document, to the lost souls, inviting them to the table. The high priest uses special finger movements borrowed from Buddhism, along with a bowl of sacred water, to transform himself into a Heavenly Worthy. With singing and chanting he passes incense over the food. At last he tosses the food he has blessed to the crowd. Finally the papier-mâché decorations and the special documents are burned in a bonfire. The festival ends.

OTHER RITUALS

Less elaborate Daoist festivals occur throughout the year. For example, on the 15th day of the Eighth Moon there is the beautiful Lantern Festival, which celebrates the bright harvest moon;

lanterns are made to reflect back the beauty of the light of the moon. This is a very popular festival for children.

DOMESTIC RITUALS

Daoists are encouraged to practice their religion on their own, without the intervention of a priest. Many Daoist homes have altars or shrines that contain their ancestor tablet, a kind of family tree. At the home altar both men and women conduct the rites for health and prosperity, for healing in times of sickness, or in memory of their ancestors. They may light incense and candles, burn offerings such as the paper ghost money that symbolizes family wealth, and chant words from the *Daozang*.

ANCESTOR RITES

Ancestor rites are very important in Chinese culture, which places a high value on family and continuity. Families will often hold private memorials for their ancestors before celebrating a festi-

Pots for holding joss-sticks and candles in front of a Daoist temple. When the joss-sticks are lit, the rising incense symbolizes prayers that are offered to Heaven.

Urns containing incense offerings in a Chinese cemetery. Graves are cleaned and fresh offerings made in early April at the festival of Qing Ming, which honors the ancestors.

val meal like the one served to welcome the new year. A simple ancestor memorial might include the burning of incense and a libation, or ritual pouring, of wine at the family altar as well as prayers in which family members share the events of the day with their ancestor and ask the ancestor's blessing.

More elaborate ancestor rites require that the home altar be arranged in a special way, with incense in the middle and flowers and candles on either side. Foodstuffs including meat, beans, fruit, soup, cookies, rice, tea, and wine are offered to the ancestors in a prescribed order. A member of the family reads an official ritual document modeled on forms in the *Daozang*. At this time the family may open the ancestor tablet and add the names of anyone who has recently died.

In early April families celebrate a festival in which they refurbish the tombs of their ancestors. They burn incense and offer wine to the ancestor spirits and make small fires in which they burn paper ghost money and other offerings. For those who have recently lost loved ones it is a time to mourn; but it is also a time to celebrate family togetherness with visits and, as is customary in all Daoist celebrations, a shared banquet.

THE CHINESE CALENDAR

As well as having their own festivals, Daoists celebrate the main Chinese festivals, as do Buddhists. The Chinese reckoning of time begins in the year 2637 B.C.E In that year, according to legend, the prime minister of the court of Huangdi, the Yellow Emperor, worked out the cycle of 60 years that is the center of the Chinese calendar, the Sexagenary Cycle. The Sexagenary Cycle is very important both in predicting the future and in recording age. A Chinese person's most important birthday is the 60th, when he or she has completed one Sexagenary Cycle.

The Sexagenary Cycle is based on the Five Elements: metal, wood, fire, earth, and water. Each element has two sides, yin and yang. These 10 sides are called the Heavenly Stems. Each stem is also associated with a color. The yang side of wood, for example, is green, and the yin side blue.

This gold medallion depicts a rooster, representing one of the
12 Earthly Branches of the Chinese calendar. Gold, a metal,
represents one of the Five Elements.

The 10 Heavenly Stems combine with 12 Earthly Branches. Each Earthly Branch is represented by an animal: monkey, rooster, dog, pig, rat, ox, tiger, rabbit, dragon, snake, horse, and goat. Thus a Chinese year is described as the Year of the Silver Goat or the Year of the Purple Monkey. It takes 60 years for an animal and a color to match again and for the cycle to be repeated.

THE DAOIST YEAR

All of the Daoist ritual celebrations are part of a regular calendar of Daoist festivals. Most festivals mark the birthday of a god or other heavenly worthy. Many important celebrations fall on or around the 15th of the lunar calendar month.

CHINESE NEW YEAR

The festival year begins with New Year's Day—the first day of the first month of the Chinese calendar. In general the first Chinese month corresponds to February on the Western calendar. On New Year's Day Daoists celebrate the rebirth of yang, the positive force of the universe, into the world. Rituals in the Daoist temples and in the homes welcome the Three Pure Ones of the Highest Heavens with an offering of sweets, or *tian* (in Chinese, *tian* means both "heaven" and "sweet"). Wooden blocks cast like dice determine when the gods have finished their banquet. When the blocks turn up together three times in a row the gods are considered to have finished their meal and to have said yes to the hopes and prayers that have been expressed. At home an ancestor offering is made and the family celebrates the coming of a new year with a banquet, gifts, the exchange of good wishes, and visits to friends and relatives.

WORSHIP AND SHRINES

The Daoist calendar provides structure but Daoists do not hold regularly scheduled worship services in the Western sense. Daoist temples and shrines are always open and someone may drop in to light incense or perhaps to pray to the gods and then draw a slip from a bamboo tube. The slip holds a prediction for the future and refers the petitioner to a book of divination. Daoist seers then interpret the message. Someone with a particularly urgent problem may consult a priest, who will perform a special temple ritual. However it is not necessary to visit a temple at all in order to be a practicing Daoist. Many small roadside shrines com-

Paper money is burned at funerals to provide support for the dead in the next world. Paper offerings are also burned at the Hungry Ghost Festival on the 15th day of the seventh lunar month, to ease the wandering souls of unsettled spirits.

memorate places where something important occurred—a place where someone was saved from falling off a cliff, for example, or where someone escaped harm in an accident. Leaving offerings at these places is a form of Daoist worship.

DAOIST RITES OF PASSAGE

As do most religious traditions, Daoism recognizes major events in life such as birth, death, and marriage. However there is little in Daoist practice that corresponds directly to rites of passage such as circumcision and bar and bat mitzvah in the Jewish tradition or baptism and confirmation in the Christian church. Rather changes in a person's life status are marked with celebrations that reinforce the individual's place in the Daoist community, the family, and the natural universe.

BIRTH AND INFANCY

Children are much honored in Chinese life as symbols of family continuity and strength. Even before birth Daoists believe a child is protected by Tai Shen, the guardian spirit of unborn children. A woman who is expecting a child will make suitable offerings to ensure a safe delivery and a healthy baby. Priests too may be asked to perform special rituals.

After the baby's birth the new mother once again makes offerings at shrines or temples. Articles of baby clothing are customary gifts to the female spirits who are themselves mothers and who look after women. A Daoist adult may be chosen to be a kind of godparent, someone who will help to keep the child safe and peaceful. Daoist charms may be used to predict what problems, if any, may beset the child and to protect him or her from harm. When the baby is one month old thanksgiving offerings of peach cakes are made

Kitchen God

At the end of the Daoist year, in one of the most widely practiced domestic rituals, the kitchen god, who has been installed in every home to observe the doings of the family, is dispatched to heaven to report to the Jade Emperor, the ruling god of the lower heavens. The kitchen god usually hangs on the kitchen wall, represented by a piece of paper that is burned to send it on its way to heaven. Soon after the coming of the New Year the kitchen god is welcomed back and the cycle begins again.

CALENDAR OF DAOIST FESTIVALS

February (First Month)

    1   New Year's Day, the Feast of the Three Pure Ones—the gods of heaven, earth, and man—who live in the highest heavens and from whom all visible things come

    4   Seeing Off the Heavenly Spirits; Welcoming Back the Kitchen God

    6   Birthday of the Jade Emperor, the ruling god of the lower heavens

    15   Festival of the Spirits of Heaven

March (Second Month)

    2   Birthday of the Lord of the Soil. This servant of the Yellow Emperor caused crops to flourish.

    16   Birthday of Laozi

    19   Birthday of Guan Yin, goddesss of compassion in Daoism and Buddhism

April (Third Month)

    23   Birthday of Sheng Mu, Empress of the Heavens

    26   Birthday of Zhang Daoling, founder of religious Daoism

May (Fourth Month)

    4   Birthday of Buddha

    14   Birthday of Lu Dongbin, or Ancestor Lu, one of the Eight Immortals

June (Fifth Month)

    5   Festival of the Summer Solstice. On this day yang is at the height of its power.

July (Sixth Month)

    28   Birthday of the God of Thunder

August (Seventh Month)

    15   Hungry Ghosts Festival, when restless sprits are free to wander and have to be appeased with offerings

September (Eighth Month)

    1   Festival of the Autumn Moon

October (Ninth Month)

    28   Birthday of Confucius

November (Tenth Month)

    10   Festival of Yu the Great, patron spirit of community renewal

    15   Birthday of the God of Water

December (Eleventh Month)

    15   Winter Solstice and Solar New Year

January (Twelfth Month)

    23–24   Return of the kitchen god to heaven

in celebration of its health and safety. Friends and relatives bring sets of baby clothes, called head-to-foot presents, and more peach cakes, which are first placed on the altar and then passed around to the family's other children. Growing children are protected by a mother spirit, or *chuang mu*. A special offering of cooked rice is made to this spirit if the child is ill or fussy. There are no specific Daoist puberty rites. A *jiao* may be made at the family altar to celebrate a young person's completing his or her studies and becoming an adult.

On the first day of the New Year festival, a dragon dance in Chinatown in Manchester, England. The dragon follows a child carrying a bright red ball, which is the symbol of yang hidden in a dark sea of yin. The dragon swallows the ball to bring long life, immortality, and union with the heavenly spirits.

DAOIST WEDDINGS

A wedding establishes the family, the center of Chinese life. The full wedding rite comes from the time of the Han dynasty (around 200 B.C.E.) and is rarely performed today. Full wedding ritual requires a formal exchange of birth dates, which are examined by a Daoist specialist. If the combination of birth dates makes an uneven, or yang, number the announcement of the wedding is presented before the family altar with an offering of incense.

The bride and groom exchange traditional gifts to seal the formal engagement, and a date is set for the wedding. The families may consult Daoist priests or fortune-tellers on questions of proper ritual and for favorable dates. They are also increasingly likely to have a full-blown "Western" wedding, with full white bridal gown and the groom in a suit or tuxedo. Then after this they will change into traditional clothes for the dragon (for the

Red lanterns hanging from the arches at the entrance to a Daoist temple. Red is considered an auspicious color in China and ritual offerings, gifts, or clothing are often colored red to bestow good fortune and prosperity.

men) and phoenix (for the women), the dragon and phoenix being symbols of male and female, yang and yin.

Following a ritual at the groom's ancestor shrine in which the groom is reminded of his duties to the bride, a procession leads him to the bride's home. The ceremony itself is simple and takes place as part of a banquet. Everyone is asked to sit down and the bride and groom drink from the wedding cup. They then sign a document of marriage and the banquet proceeds. The next day the bride traditionally goes to the home of her husband's parents. She carries with her gifts that symbolize her intent to bear children for the family and she worships at her husband's ancestor tablet. Three days after the wedding the bride visits her own parents. Her visit signifies that she is now a member of another family and that she is a visitor in her former home.

First Birthday Celebrations

On a baby's first birthday the parents celebrate his or her safe passage through the first year of life with a banquet for the neighborhood. The baby is offered a tray with items symbolizing different paths in life—hard work, intelligence, wealth, health, and scholarship, for example—and given its first bite of solid food. Finally the baby gets a sweet rice cake to turn his or her thoughts from worldly to heavenly things.

DAOIST FUNERALS

Daoists believe that at death the *shen,* or spirit, separates from the body but remains nearby until the body is buried. Then that part of the spirit that governs passions, grief, and other strong feelings is buried with the body. The pure spiritual essence of the person survives and goes on either to peaceful rest or to face punishment from the gods for misdeeds on earth.

The good works of the living and proper ritual can buy the dead person a reprieve from divine punishment. Funerals therefore are as lavish as a family can afford. Correct observance of Daoist funeral rites is so important to Daoists that an entire branch of the priesthood oversees it. Today these are the "blackhead" Daoists, so called for their black headdresses. The service for the dead can last from one to three days and includes Daoist music, ritual, and chants.

Elaborate rules regulate the care of the dying person, the actions of the caregivers at the time of death, and preparation of the body for the funeral. A Daoist priest is often summoned to oversee the preparations in the home and make sure that they are ritually correct.

BANQUET FOR THE DEAD

The family altar and its decorations are covered with a white cloth, the color of yin or sadness. The body is placed in the coffin and the children of the family are invited to put the deceased's favorite things in with it. Children perform this service because they do not know the monetary value of things and will therefore choose truly, without thought of cost. The family prepares a banquet and puts the dead person's favorite foods in the coffin as well as special charms or prayers written on slips of white paper. While the priest chants the ritual for the dead the slips of paper are taken from the coffin and burned as offerings to send them to heaven, and new charms are added. When the ritual is complete the coffin is sealed and a banquet follows.

GUIDING THE SPIRIT TO REST

The burial day is determined by a Daoist calendar specialist, who chooses a favorable day for the event. On that day a procession of priests, musicians, and mourners makes its way to the cemetery. The Daoist priests walk in front of the coffin shaking bells, playing their instruments, and saying magic spells. These activities help to guide the dead person's spirit to its rest. So from birth to death Daoist rituals and festivals shape the lives of Daoist believers and work to keep them in harmony with the rhythms of the universe.

MEDITATION

The center of priestly life and of all Daoist practice is meditation. The basis for Daoist meditation can be found in the *Daodejing,* in which Chapter 16 begins, "Empty your mind of all thoughts." It has been said that someone can learn meditation in a day but must

A family making offerings at a grave in a Hong Kong cemetery. The family of the deceased regularly visit the grave to offer food, incense, and flowers, particularly at the festival of Qing Ming. Daoists believe that the actions of the living can help the spirits of the dead rest peacefully.

One with the Great Void

Early Daoist masters took up the recommendation of Laozi to empty the mind of all thoughts and commented on it. The *Zhuangzi* records the words of a master named Yen Hui, who said this about meditation: "My connection with my body and all its parts is dissolved. Seeing and hearing are discarded. Thus leaving my material form, and quitting all my knowledge, I become one with the Great Void. This I call sitting and forgetting."

practice it for a lifetime in order to understand it fully. There are various levels of Daoist meditation. Only the most skilled students ever reach the highest plane, in which they are united with Dao. At its simplest levels students learn to empty their minds of all desires and emotions, all thoughts and wishes, and to channel spiritual energy within the body.

One of the things that students of meditation practice is breath control. In Daoist understanding breathing does not simply mean the passage of air into and out of the lungs. In Daoist interpretation breathing includes the way oxygen is carried to parts of the body in the bloodstream by the circulatory system and waste products are carried away. Daoists try to harness the energy of the breath, or *qi*, and guide it through the body by concentration. Eventually they become adept at directing oxygen to places that might be hurting so that they can be healed. As Daoists advance in technique they turn this process too over to the unconscious. They can then let the energizing *qi* go where it wants to go.

Taijiquan, an early Daoist system of exercises developed as an aid to learning meditation, helps people channel *qi* around their bodies before they are able to do it with concentration alone. The goal of the exercises in concentration and meditation is to achieve "embryonic breathing." This is described as the way energy is transmitted effortlessly to the body of an unborn child. The whole process is one of physical and spiritual development, or "inner alchemy." At its end the Daoist's vitality, energy, and spirit become one with Dao.

VISUALIZING THE GODS

Another form of meditation requires students to visualize the gods of true life. This allows the gods to enter into a person and brings their blessings of life into the body. By visualizing the sun, the moon, the planets, the stars, and the heavenly gods an individual can crowd out the demons of anger, suspicion, envy, and annoyance that wear down energy. Visualizing the gods brings people back to their natural state. It allows the gods to enter and set up their own presence within.

Learning Daoist meditation can take many years—even a lifetime. Students must give up all motivation and desire, even the desire to learn how to meditate or to have meditation "work." They must renounce all sense of individual identity and become totally absorbed in meditating for its own sake. In so doing they become one with Dao, like water that is poured into water. Entering into the rhythms of nature they find within themselves the inner light that is Dao.

CHAPTER 6

THE DAO AND THE ARTS

Zhuangzi tells the story of a master carver who had to forget himself and all he had to gain in order to create an almost perfect bell stand. He had to let Dao take over. Once he came into harmony with the nature of the tree, the beautiful bell stand emerged from the wood without effort on his part.

Zhuangzi's story illustrates how the creative force of Dao can work in people who let it come into their minds and bodies. The idea of finding a "way"—Dao—to produce great art effortlessly, like the master carver, has always interested creative people. Daoism appealed to Chinese painters and poets, dancers and musicians. Eventually there came to be a Daoist "way" of doing these things. It became part of many Chinese art forms.

DAO AND LITERATURE

The early Daoists produced many forms of writing besides scripture and commentaries on Daoist philosophy. Essays, stories, parables, and satire appear in early Daoist manuscripts. Many Chinese folktales, fairy tales, fables, and romances from ancient

A traditional storyteller holds the attention of the audience as he reveals a Daoist legend at Bai Yun Guan —the White Cloud temple fair in Beijing. Characters from the stories are drawn on the backdrop to the stage where actors will also perform some of the stories.

times contain elements of magic and mystery that can be linked to Daoism. During the Tang dynasty all forms of art flourished, including literature. Writers told stories of time travel, ghostly worlds, and distant magical kingdoms, all showing a clear expression of the creative, magical side of Daoism.

DAOIST POETRY

Poetry, however, was the literary form that Daoism influenced most strongly. The *Daodejing*, the foundation of Daoist scripture and thought, is a long poem. The *Daodejing* and other poems of the early Daoist sages were admired and imitated from ancient times.

Between the third and the seventh centuries C.E. Daoist and Buddhist beliefs about nature inspired new ways of treating nature in poetry. Reverence for nature became a major theme, along with human relationships and a longing for the past.

The poet Dao Qian (Dao Ch'ien) (372–427 C.E.) was considered the finest poet of his time. A Confucian official, he became drawn to Daoism. Eventually he left his job with the court to live in and write about the world of nature. Many of his poems express the joy he felt in becoming one with nature, which is a Daoist ideal. Here Dao Qian expresses how that can be done even in the city:

I have built my hut beside a busy road
But I can hear no clatter from passing carts and horses.
Do you want to know how?
When the mind is detached, where you are is remote also.
Picking chrysanthemums by the east hedge

I can see the hills to the south a long way away:
It is sunset and the air over the mountains is beautiful;
Birds are flying in flocks back to their nests.
This tastes real. I would like to talk about it, but
there are no words.
(In Alasdair Clayre, *The Heart of the Dragon*.)

POETRY IN THE TANG AND SONG DYNASTIES

Poetry, like other art forms, flowered under the rule of the Tang emperors. This period became known as China's golden age of poetry (618–907). Many poems from this time are celebrations of nature. Often they suggest that natural wonders are hints of the divine world.

One of the best-known poets of the age was a Daoist named Li Bai (Li Po, 701–62). Li Bai wrote more than 1,000 poems. Many of them center on the natural life of the Daoist and living at one with the natural world.

Life during the Tang period was, however, far from serene. There was almost constant rebellion and warfare. In trying to understand the meaning of life in times that were often cruel and brutal, many Tang poets turned to Daoism. Thinking about the beauties of nature offered an escape from war's horrors. Like the poems of others in his time, many of Li Bai's poems reflect the world he lived in and saw.

SU DONGPO

Another of China's greatest poets was Su Dongpo (Su Tong-p'o), who lived during the Song dynasty (960–1279). Su was a Confucian scholar-official who worked

MOON OVER MOUNTAIN PASS

Even the war poems of Li Bai contain images of the natural world:

A bright moon rising above Tian Shan
Lost in a vast ocean of clouds.
The long wind, across thousands upon
*   thousands of miles.*
Blows past the Jade-gate Pass.
The army of Han has gone down the
*   Pai-teng Road,*
As the barbarian hordes probe at
*   Ch'ing-hai Bay.*
It is known that from the battlefield Few
*   ever live to return.*
Men at garrison look on the
*   border scene.*
Home thoughts deepen sorrow on
*   their faces.*
In the towered chambers tonight,
Ceaseless are the women's sighs.

(In Wuji Liu and Irving Yucheng Lo, *Sunflower Splendor*.)

for the government. In fact he gained fame as one of China's finest administrators. He wrote many official documents in clear, practical, Confucian prose. His mother was a Daoist, however, and Su had a Daoist education. As he grew older he was attracted to Buddhism. These three traditions blended in his poetry.

Daoism encouraged a lack of restraint and an openness to beauty that released a creative spirit in many poets. Together with the Daoist sensitivity to the natural world, it left a lasting mark on centuries of Chinese poetry.

DAOISM AND PAINTING

Even more than poetry Chinese painting became an expression of Dao. According to one of the early Daoist paradoxes Dao could not be expressed by either words or silence. To Daoists painting helped to explain how that might be possible. Painting is neither words nor silence, yet it communicates ideas and truths about nature and the universe. The poet Su Dongpo, who was also a painter, referred to paintings as "silent poems."

Painting in China began in the temples. Monks and priests drew the patterns of the sun, the moon, and the stars as part of their religious rituals. Later monks and nuns practiced painting as a devotional exercise. The concentration required for painting was a way of focusing the mind on the harmony of the natural world. Even after its purpose was no longer strictly religious, the basic aim of painting was still to express the Chinese belief in universal order and harmony of Dao.

In the fifth century a Chinese art critic named Xie Ho (Hsieh Ho) established six canons, or rules, for the creation of truly great art. According to Xie Ho, five of whose canons dealt with technique, form, color, composition, and the preservation of Chinese tradition, a painting must have *qi*—that is, energy, the breath of life. The sixth canon indicated that *qi* could not be acquired simply by practice and study; it had to come from within. Thus Chinese painters looked on painting not as a profession but as a way of life. They worked for years to develop the muscular control necessary to make the sure, swift, delicate strokes that would infuse their paintings with *qi*. Xie Ho's rules had set the standards for Chinese art for centuries to come.

CLASSICAL PAINTERS: BALANCING THE ELEMENTS

The classical painters strove to achieve union with the Dao through their subject matter. A painting was not a literal representation of a scene but a blending of what the artist saw and the way the artist's mind transformed it. The most important factor was that the breath of life should appear in every form.

Wang Wei (699–759) was the landscape painter of his age whose work best captured the essence of *qi*. A Daoist, he drew strength and inspiration from nature. "Gazing upon the clouds of autumn, my spirit takes wings and soars," he wrote. "Facing the breeze of spring, my thoughts flow like great, powerful currents." He wrote of looking at a well-executed painting: "The wind rises from the green forest, and the foaming water rushes in the stream. Alas! Such painting cannot be achieved by physical movements of the fingers and hand, but only by the spirit entering into them. This is the nature of painting." The paintings themselves

CREATIVE FORCE OF DAO

The goal of a painter was to reach a level of true inspiration, a union with Dao. Like the meditating monks and nuns of the Daoist monasteries, painters tried to achieve a state in which their hearts and minds were emptied, their spirits freed, and their bodies prepared so that the creative force could work through them. In one of his poems Su Dongpo tells of learning to paint from his friend Yuko:

When Yuko painted bamboo,
He saw bamboo, not himself.
Nor was he simply unconscious
   of himself:
Trancelike, he left his body.
His body was transformed into
   bamboo,
Creating inexhaustible freshness . . .

(In Alasdair Clayre, *The Heart of the Dragon*.)

A painting of the three sages of Taiji surrounded by symbols of long life and immortality—a tree, a deer, and a peach. The yin-yang symbol is in the center of the scroll they are holding. The sages have been placed in a natural mountain setting in keeping with the nature of the Dao.

adhered to the principle of yin and yang, the opposing forces that balance each other in the natural world. Landscape painters in particular worked to achieve a perfect balance of elements through composition. Mountains and foothills were balanced by rivers and streams, and long views of land by clouds and trees.

CAPTURING ENDLESS CHANGE

Painters hoped to capture the feeling of endless change and motion and the cycles of life that were basic to Daoism. In keeping with the principle of *qi,* they felt that landscapes should never seem still. Paintings were often done on long scrolls that were unrolled a little at a time to display a constantly changing perspective. Tiny figures or buildings in the landscape symbolized the unimportance of human beings in the universe.

"His mountains soared and his springs flowed," it was said of Wang Wei. "To paint mountains," Wang wrote, "one must first know their spiritual forms." His Daoist approach to painting had a profound effect on succeeding generations of artists. A thousand years later in 1701 the classic Chinese how-to book of painting, *Mustard Seed Garden Manual,* held up his style as a model for aspiring painters.

FLASH OF INSPIRATION

The classic style of painting continued to have great influence into the modern age, but other forms of painting also expressed Daoist ideas. In the south of China in the 12th-century Daoist thought influenced the Chan Buddhists and gave rise to another form of painting. The Daoist and Chan Buddhist painters believed that inspiration often came in a flash and left as quickly. They turned away from the practiced, thoughtful style of the northern painters and experimented with more spontaneous forms. They drew with

A Harmonious Mind

Although Daoist ideals are most clearly expressed in landscape painting, they can be found in other subjects as well. The Chinese are famous for their graceful drawings and paintings of forms in nature. These subjects, like others, were held to the standard of *qi,* the life force. Whatever they were painting artists were reminded to set their minds on the harmony of the universe.

whatever was at hand—one artist was said to have used his cap dipped in ink—and finished the details later. A frequent subject was the dragon, a Daoist symbol because of its great force and its magical qualities.

MODERN CHINESE ART

Today Chinese students of painting still follow the six canons laid down by Xie Ho in the fifth century. They work to acquire the technique of brushstrokes, coloration, and form that have governed Chinese painting for centuries, often combining it with rapid-ink

An eighth-century painting from the Tang Dynasty called *Two Horses and a Groom* by the artist Han Gan. The artist was famous during his lifetime and in succeeding generations for his paintings of horses.

and Western techniques. Among China's artists nature remains a popular subject, still an important element of Chinese culture and part of the Daoist legacy.

DAO AND CALLIGRAPHY

Chinese painting is closely linked to another ancient art form, that of calligraphy, or the writing of Chinese characters. Both developed classical styles during the Tang dynasty, and both have many similarities. Since calligraphy and painting use the same materials—brush and ink—and both are based on line and form, many painters practiced calligraphy to help train their hands and eyes for painting. However calligraphy is an art in its own right. Examples of fine Chinese writing are considered valuable works of art today.

Asleep on a Tiger

One of the early "rapid ink" drawings—a drawing done spontaneously as Daoist and Chan Buddhist painters believed that inspiration often comes in a flash and left as quickly—clearly demonstrates Daoist influence. Entitled *Two Minds in Harmony,"* the drawing shows an old man asleep, leaning on the back of a sleeping tiger. The painting, which is believed to have been drawn with a bunch of straw dipped in ink, illustrates the basic Daoist belief in the harmony between human beings and nature.

LIVING MOVEMENT

Calligraphers try to make their writing appear as if it had grown naturally. They attempt to give it *qi*, which they define as "the kind of life inherent in mountains, streams, and trees." Well-formed characters are said to have "bone" and to be "sinewy." They appear lean and muscular, not flabby and soft, or "dead."

In order for a character to have *qi*, every stroke in it must convey a sense of living movement. The Chinese feel that looking at a fine piece of calligraphy should be like watching a dancer perform. In both arts rhythm, line, and form are blended into a harmonious whole that reflects the harmony of the universe.

Each character must also be balanced. Its yin and yang, or weak and strong, elements must fit together into a tightly knit whole. Along with this it must be "centered." It is not enough to make perfect strokes; the space between the strokes must be controlled so that the character holds together visually. All of these concepts

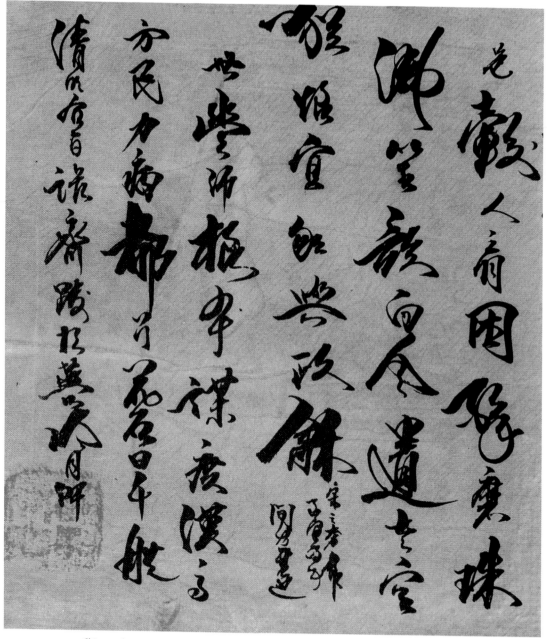

Chinese characters are pictographic; originally the characters were simple line drawings of objects. To a calligrapher every line and dot suggests the form of something in nature. Thus the natural world is considered an important inspiration for calligraphy. In classical Chinese art calligraphy, painting, and poetry often appear together on one scroll. The interplay of the words in the poem, the design of the characters, and the figures and forms of the painting enrich one another, creating the sense of harmony in the universe that is Dao.

are closely related to Daoist ideas of balance and harmony.

THE DISCIPLINE OF CALLIGRAPHY

Fine calligraphy takes many years to learn. In addition to the arm, fingers, and wrist, the whole body is involved in creating and controlling strokes. Manuals on calligraphy explain that the posture must be upright and balanced—calligraphers usually stand when they work—the wrist suspended above the paper, and the mind concentrated. Breathing is controlled and its energy channeled within the body. In China calligraphy is considered to be a healthful exercise that contributes to longevity, as physical an activity as walking, jogging, or swimming.

The discipline needed for calligraphy is similar to that needed for meditation. From at least the fourth century of the common era Daoist monks learned it as part of their devotional practice and used it to copy sacred texts. It was yet another way of focusing the mind and body on Dao. Even today calligraphers try to empty their minds and write in a state of mental calm like the tranquillity of the ancient Daoist monks.

HUANG TINGJIAN

Classical calligraphers turned to the work of earlier writers for inspiration. Huang Tingjian (Huang T'ing-chien) (1045–1105) was a calligrapher of the Song period (960–1260) whose work helped to bring new style and vitality to his art. A revolutionary who was forced to endure exile, he used sixth- and eighth-century Daoist texts for models. He believed that copying these texts would be "an elixir that transforms iron into gold," a kind of mental tonic. Huang was described as following through each stroke with his whole body, alternately lifting and pressing down on the brush to form strokes full of individuality and life. The force of his personality combined with ritual and nature to produce work of lasting beauty and power.

DAOIST MUSIC

In the 17th-century painter Wang Yuanqi wrote, "The Dao or 'way' of music is interchangeable with that of painting." Daoists understood music to be a part of the harmony of the universe. Both instrumental music and song are an essential part of Daoist ritual.

Daoist ritual music varied from sect to sect and from area to area. In some parts of the country percussion instruments like drums, bells, cymbals, and gongs were favored. Other areas

ZHAI JIAO

The ancient Daoist ritual Zhai Jiao (Chai Chiao) is used to make offerings to the gods for immortality. The song that accompanies it describes how the gods help people overcome the demons that bring natural disasters. It is played on traditional Chinese musical instruments, including a flute, a two-stringed fiddle, a Chinese mandolin, and a harp. In form and sound the song merges its own region's Chinese folk music and ballads with imperial court music. It is intended to produce feelings of calm and peace, in keeping with Daoist philosophy.

developed traditions using oboes, flutes, and strings, or combinations of percussion and wind instruments.

PASSING ON HEAVENLY MUSIC

Traditionally Daoist music was never written down. It was considered "heavenly music," a ritual form to be passed on by priests to the next generation of musicians. During China's Cultural Revolution (1966–76) the government attacked many of China's intellectuals and artists for their views. Daoist music was banned along with all religious practice. Priests and monks were persecuted for practicing religion in any way. A few Daoist priests defied the ban. They struggled to keep the tradition of Daoist music alive by playing in secret, often in caves or in remote mountain areas. However until recently the knowledge of Daoist music was in grave danger of dying out. The opening of China to the West, however, brought with it a new interest in Chinese culture, including Daoist music.

REDISCOVERY AND RECORDINGS

Professors of music at Chinese universities have been leading the drive to locate and record Daoist music before the people who know it are gone. They have been videotaping priests who remember the music, now very old men, and making transcripts so that others can learn it. The tradition is being passed on to younger priests and to musicians. The music of some rituals is now available in bookstores in Hong Kong and in China.

A rarity in the past, religious music events are now found throughout China. Daoist music societies often sponsor such gatherings, as do local and provincial governments. The increasing visibility of traditional Chinese music may be due to the reforming Communist government's new religion policy. The government now recognizes traditional religious music as an important part of China's cultural heritage.

THE DAO OF DANCE

Like music, dance is also a part of Daoist ritual. Priests follow the traditional patterns of ancient dances as they chant Daoist liturgy. The circling movements of the ritual dances are believed to bring worshippers into harmony with the natural cycles of the universe. Often the priests will dance a constellation of the heavens, stepping as it were from star to star in beautiful sweeping movements and high steps. These "magic circles" are repeated in ritual swordplay, in which the priest or master wields a sword to drive away evil spirits, and in the graceful movements of Taijiquan, both of which have devotional value for the Daoist.

DAOISM AND ARTISTIC EXPRESSION

For centuries Daoism has been linked with the creative forces of the natural world. It has always encouraged freedom and individuality, a close observation and acceptance of nature, a sense of harmony, and an awareness of beauty. In addition it has stressed disciplines that channel vitality and energy along creative lines. Daoists have always been among China's finest artists and poets. Their contributions have greatly enriched Chinese culture.

In the past decade the Western world has begun to examine the Daoist principles of concentration, relaxation, and physical training to enhance performance in the arts. Both Chinese and Western painters, singers, players of musical instruments, and other artists, are exploring ancient Daoist practices to give their work *qi*, or energy. In so doing they parallel the efforts of Daoists to control and direct the energy of the natural universe in everyday life.

CHAPTER 7

DAOISM YESTERDAY, TODAY, AND TOMORROW

Throughout its long tradition in China Daoism's fate has ebbed and flowed. Periods of influence were followed by ages of repression. Despite times of imperial patronage, Daoism was usually on the outside of official channels of power and sometimes in the opposition. If Confucianism was the religion of official China, then Daoism was the religion of unofficial China, the "religion of the people." In its long history Daoism has often been on the verge of extinction. The 20th century marked another challenging period in Daoism's storied history.

TURBULENCE IN THE TWENTIETH CENTURY

In 1911 the last Chinese empire fell. In the new republic that replaced it the role of religion and traditional Chinese thought was unclear. Some believed that the best of China's ancient culture deserved reappropriation and scrutiny, while others were convinced that China's only hope lay in imitating the West. As

Pilgrims and tourists visiting one of the shrines at the Hanging Temple on northern Heng Shan sacred mountain in Shanxi Province. Within the temple, dating from the fifth century, there are 40 wooden halls and structures linked by pillars and walkways.

part of the movement for national renewal in 1917, a great deal of property of state religious organizations was confiscated in what became known as the "Fourth May Movement." Many temples were turned into schools in an attempt to provide education for the poorest. By the 1930s great political forces were presenting further challenges to the region. Imperial Japan invaded China in 1937, destroying Daoist temples, priceless ancient literature, and artifacts.

COMMUNIST TAKEOVER

The tumult of the Japanese invasion, and then of the struggle against the Japanese occupation and a civil war, was soon followed by the 1949 Communist takeover. Led by Mao Zedong, the Communists made no secret of their disdain for all religion. By the 1950s it was possible for one Chinese scholar to assert Daoism's certain extinction: its vitality was sapped, its schools were in decline, its priesthood was disorganized, it lacked organization and a social program, and, dominated by the search for earthly blessings, it had lost its vision. Daoism's influence, in the opinion of many, had been reduced to art, rituals, and festivals.

RENEWAL AND RESTORATION

China has been ravaged by war and revolutions, and its inhabitants have often been caught in the middle of powerful forces largely beyond their control. Despite all this, as in ages past, Daoism has survived. Now into a new century, its future is in no way assured. Yet there are hopeful signs that after a turbulent and destructive era Daoism is enjoying a period of renewal and restoration. Daoist centers once closed are reopening and being refurbished or renovated; temples once destroyed are being rebuilt; teachings believed to have been lost forever only 20 years ago are being passed on to a new generation. The Chinese government's new policy toward religion, adopted in 1979, promises continued growth for religion in China, including Daoism. In the West Daoism in its traditional form and in the sciences it produced is finding new adherents.

A photograph of Mao Zedong taken in July 1966 during the time of the Cultural Revolution when he initiated campaigns to root out traditional Chinese culture. During his three decades in power Mao attempted to systematically eliminate all religion in China.

Chinese New Year celebrations and prayers in a temple in Qingdao, a seaport in Shandong Province. After years of neglect, many temples like this one are being renovated and returned to clergy for their proper religious use.

DAOISM UNDER COMMUNISM

After World War II (1939–45) China was seized by a violent civil war between the Nationalist government and Communist rebels. In 1949 Mao and the Communists emerged victorious, establishing the People's Republic. The Nationalists fled to the island of Taiwan. As we will see, even while Daoism appeared to diminish in the mainland after 1949, it continued as before, unthreatened, in Taiwan.

In the eyes of the Communists religion was an "opiate of the people," unscientific and therefore outdated. Religion was largely suppressed, perceived as a potential threat to the state and a subversive influence over the people. As a result all religious affairs in China were placed under the Chinese Communist Party. In 1954 the Religious Affairs Bureau (RAB) was created to supervise all religious activities. Three years later the Chinese Daoist Association was formed to regulate the religious life of Chinese Daoists.

EXPULSION AND LABOR CAMPS

In the 1950s during the Land Reform movement, Daoist temples lost much of their property, which weakened them economically. Severe restrictions on religious life were introduced. As part of the Great Leap Forward of 1958, ancient and priceless artifacts like temple bells and cauldrons were melted down to produce iron for a country crazy to modernize at nearly any cost. Many of the temples that survived were requisitioned as army barracks or government offices or became factories, workshops, or grain stores. Most festivals were officially forbidden by the government and many traditional Daoist practices such as fortune-telling and exorcism were dismissed as mere superstition.

THE CULTURAL REVOLUTION

The situation worsened during the Cultural Revolution, a decade-long campaign designed by Mao Zedong to reinstill the revolutionary fervor of the past, to destabilize the then-entrenched Chinese Communist Party, and finally to root out traditional Chinese culture. Ardent young Maoists called Red Guards went

SPIRITUAL CULTURE OF HARMONY

In recent years the Chinese government has begun to reach out to both Daoism and Buddhism. Alarmed at the culture of greed and selfishness that it has created through the single-child policy and the rise of consumerist capitalism, it has asked the ancient faiths to help create a "Spiritual Culture of Harmony." It remains to be seen if the government really wants a serious engagement with Daoism and whether Daoism trusts the government enough to wish to work that closely with it. However it marks a remarkable shift from just 30 to 40 years ago.

A community gathered at a temple to celebrate a festival linked to their town god in Shaanxi Province.

on a nationwide rampage. Youth were exhorted to denounce the so-called Four Olds: old customs, old culture, old habits, and old thinking. Daoists were tortured, killed, or sent off to labor camps. With rare exceptions almost all the Daoist centers were destroyed and surviving followers were scattered. Beginning in 1964 the Cultural Revolution seemed to complete the destruction that earlier antireligious crusades had begun.

DAOISM UNDER THE RELIGIOUS FREEDOM CLAUSE

Deng Xiaoping, Mao's successor who lead China in the 1970s and 1980s, ushered in a new era of social and cultural change under the banner of "Reform and Opening." The Religious Freedom Clause of the 1982 constitution now allows for the "right of religious belief." Religion in a rapidly modernizing China is now said to share the goals of the Communist state: morality, ethics, loyalty to China, and increased productivity. The religious reforms have had the effect of reviving religious practices throughout the country. However the government continues to maintain a tight grip on religion and still suppresses many groups, ever fearful that they might threaten the stability of the government and the nation if left unchecked.

As odd as it may sound, until the new era ushered in by Deng Xiaoping few really knew if Daoism had survived the Cultural Revolution. China, as in ages past, had become mostly closed to the West. It is now known that Daoism is experiencing a renaissance. Beginning in the 1980s temples and monasteries were reopened, first to tourists then to their priests and nuns, for proper religious use. Daoist religious leaders were called out of retirement or were allowed to leave the work camps they had been forced into during the Cultural Revolution.

Daoism and the Environment

One area where Daoists have become both active and at times critical of the government is the issue of the environment. Because of the deep respect for nature—Dao—that lies at the heart of Daoism they have been increasingly active in the last 10 to 15 years in developing their own environmental policy. In 2007 Laozi was officially declared the god of the environment by the China Daoist Association. This is one area where government and Daoists may be able to work together in the future.

New fund-raising initiatives were started in China and abroad to rebuild Daoist centers throughout China. The Chinese Daoist Association, dissolved during the Cultural Revolution, was reestablished in 1983. One year later the Bai Yun Guan (White Cloud) Temple, the largest Daoist temple in northern China, was reopened. Such restorative activities continued into the 1990s and persist today. While the number of reopened or rebuilt temples is still a fraction of what once existed, many of these places are now bustling with activity. Traditional practices, funerals, festivals, divination and pilgrimage are back.

DAOISM BEYOND THE PEOPLE'S REPUBLIC

Daoism is not confined to the People's Republic of China. Daoists can be found in Cambodia among the ethnic Chinese population. In Singapore 8.5 percent of the country's 4.6 million describe themselves as Daoists. Recently Singaporean Daoist leaders proclaimed Laozi's birthday, the 15th day of the second lunar month, Daoist Day, with the hope that the celebration will catch on among Daoists throughout the world.

Until 1997 Hong Kong was a colony of the United Kingdom. Many feared that the handover of control to Communist China would limit religious freedom, but this has not been the case. The Chinese Daoist Association has chapters in all provinces and major cities. It promotes Daoism through support of the education of children and adults, sponsors Daoist functions throughout Hong Kong, and supports the growth and development of Daoism on the mainland. As in other parts of China there are many Daoist groups and practices, and Daoism is often practiced together with Buddhism and/or Confucianism. Daoist and Buddhist deities are present in 600 Chinese temples in Hong Kong. Daoism's strongest presence outside mainland China is in Taiwan. During the Cultural Revolution the island was the most visible center for open Daoist practice. The home-in-exile of the Celestial Master, the island boasts 7.6 million followers. With such a thriving Daoist community Taiwan has long been a center of Daoist study, exchange, and scholarship.

DAOISM IN THE WEST

Although Daoism has not been as popular as Buddhism and Confucianism outside of Asia, there are now Daoist communities in nearly every major Western city. The increased presence of Eastern religions among native Westerners comes at a time when many are looking beyond the traditional religions of the Occident. Eager to seek new answers to old questions and novel solutions to the problems of modern society, they are often more receptive to these faiths and philosophies than they are to the religions of their parents or grandparents. In a shrinking world where Daoists meditate in North America and Roman Catholics worship in Korea, the very terms *East* and *West* are not as clear as they once were.

North American Daoism

An example of Western Daoism can be found in Weston, Massachusetts. The Center of Traditional Daoist studies is led by a Western master who regularly conducts rituals in a temple filled with traditional Daoist deities. Courses are taught in Daoist religion, philosophy, Taijiquan, and martial arts. The center is recognized by the ancient White Cloud Temple of Shanghai and by Shanghai Quan Shen Daoists, a significant affirmation of its authenticity. Such places are still few in number but their presence reflects both Western interest in Daoism and the growth of religious pluralism in North America, where some 30,000 people identify themselves as Daoists.

TECHNIQUES AND PRACTICES

While the number of Western Daoist initiates remains small, interest in Daoist techniques and practices is increasing. When one goes to the "Eastern Religions" section of a neighborhood bookstore or local library today, he or she will see books dealing with the Dao of science, singing, or health. Fritjof Capra's 1975 publication of the *Tao of Physics* began this trend. Capra examines the similarities between physics and Daoism, both disciplines that try to understand the natural laws of the universe.

Another intriguing book is the *Tao of Pooh* by Benjamin Hoff. One may be surprised to find out that A. A. Milne's Winnie the Pooh is the prototypical Daoist! Pooh's simplicity, contentment, compassion, and wisdom make him the perfect Western embodiment of the *Daodejing*. Such books represent serious attempts to apply Daoist concepts, philosophies, and traditions to modern Western life.

ACUPUNCTURE

Acupuncture is a medical art with Daoist roots that is having an increasing influence on Western society. Acupuncturists insert tiny needles into the surface of the body to improve physiological functions. Like Taijiquan acupuncture is based on the assumption that the body is animated by *qi*, or energy, and that blockages to this energy produce illness. Acupuncture aims to restore equilibrium, the proper flow, and continuity to the flow of *qi* through manipulation of the meridians (pathways of energy) in the body. Over the last decade the Western medical community has acknowledged acupuncture's effectiveness in the alleviation of pain, but there is still reluctance to admit its success in treating arthritis, depression, and nicotine addiction—other ailments that acupuncturists commonly treat. In some states in the United States only medical doctors are allowed to practice acupuncture.

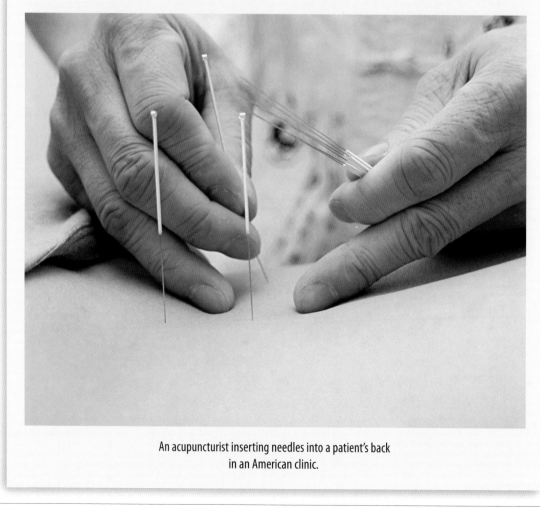

An acupuncturist inserting needles into a patient's back
in an American clinic.

ASIAN MEDICINE

Over the last 30 years Daoism has influenced the West through the growing popularity of Asian medicine, especially Taijiquan, acupuncture, and herbal therapies. In general Asian medicine is characterized by its attention to the whole person rather than to localized symptoms, as is often the case in traditional Western medicine.

Scholars consider Taiji the ancestor of all Chinese martial arts. Because it involves stretching and extension exercises it is useful to people of all ages and physical conditions. Many Westerners now practice Taiji because they find that it reduces body pains, alleviates tension, and improves circulation.

It is no longer unusual to find a herbal medicine section at the local grocery store, or a Chinese traditional medicine clinic or pharmacy in the center of a major town or city in the West. What many do not realize when they buy ginkgo biloba or ginseng is that such treatments have their roots in Asia. Western science still categorizes herbal medicines as "untested." However in the years ahead it is likely that Daoism-developed medical arts will become more common and will be incorporated into traditional Western therapies. There are already 17 universities in the United States that offer courses in Asian medicine, and many other schools from the West Coast to the East and throughout Western Europe are dedicated to what is often termed complementary and alternative medicine.

DAOISM INTO THE FUTURE

What might Daoism look like in the years ahead? Because most have been wrong in their religious predictions perhaps the temptation to pass quick judgments or to offer simplistic prophesies should be resisted. The best way to forecast Daoism's future is probably to observe what is taking place today. Fueled by the liberalizing policies of the People's Republic of China, temples and monasteries throughout the mainland are being rebuilt, attendance at Daoist festivals in China are the highest they have been in three generations, and Daoist masters are emerging from exile to teach interested new disciples the ancient ways and beliefs of the Celestial Masters.

INTERNATIONAL COOPERATION

As recently as the mid-20th century Daoism was declared dead, due in part to the decline of its schools. Today Daoist studies take place in religious organizations like the Chinese Daoist Association, in institutions of higher learning such as Beijing University, in research institutes such as the Chinese Academy of Social Sciences, and in cultural and artistic institutions such as the Ethnology Institute. By the mid-20th century the Daoist priesthood was deemed disorganized. Since 1979 the few elderly Daoists still living have begun the process of educating new followers, restoring ancient manuscripts, and reorganizing monastic life. Despite obstacles they have been largely successful in creating a network of cooperation throughout Asia and the West.

In the mid-20th century most Westerners knew almost nothing of Daoism or its constituent arts. Today, as we have seen, there is widespread interest in the *Daodejing* and the *Yijing*; many seek the benefits of Asian medicine and Taijiquan; and Daoist organizations in North America and Europe are working to preserve and restore China's Daoist heritage. These are promising signs and a helpful indicator of Daoism's continued renewal in the new century.

THREATS TO DAOIST HERITAGE

Of course Daoist history, like Daoist teaching, is a reminder that times of hardship will naturally follow prosperity. The future is in no way certain. The Communist government still supervises all the religions of China and often represses "unofficial" groups it deems potentially subversive and unpatriotic—for example the suppression of Buddhists in Tibet prior to the Olympic Games in Beijing in 2008. While the government claims that Daoism shares its goals, in truth it is more accurate to say that the government allows "the people's religion" as long as it appears to support the government's agenda. This agenda could quickly change.

A boy and his father at a Daoist temple in Shatin, Hong Kong. At temples and shrines, offerings are made and ancestors venerated.

While hundreds of temples are being rebuilt and others are being handed back to priests, many more remain government offices, workshops, or factories. Historic Daoist centers like Mount Mao near Nanjing or one of the five great sacred mountains of Daoism such as Hua Shan near Xian —places destroyed, rebuilt, and destroyed again over the last three centuries—now face a new enemy: uncontrolled tourism. While visitors provide the monks and nuns with their main source of income, they also threaten their ability to continue an ascetic (self-denying) lifestyle. Those centers not returned to the masters are often transformed into theme parks.

People pray for good fortune at New Year celebrations at the White Cloud Temple in Beijing. They will toss their handfuls of burning incense sticks into a large fire.

SURVIVAL AND THE FUTURE

Like many Chinese intellectuals a century ago, many Chinese now reject religious aspects of Daoism as backward. Young people eager to embrace the benefits of China's new economy are often unwilling to embrace a life of contemplation and self-denial. As a result ancient knowledge, practices, and skills will die with old Daoist practitioners, forever lost because there was simply no one willing to receive them.

However a surprising revival is beginning to take place as young people, frustrated by the consumerism of contemporary China, seek something of more substance. For now at least Daoism is enjoying a period of renewal. Against incredible odds and despite wars, suppression, killing, and scorn, Daoism has survived. It is a startling reality perhaps best captured by these verses from *Daodejing*:

Nothing in the world
is as soft and yielding as water.
Yet for dissolving the hard and inflexible,
Nothing can surpass it.
The soft overcomes the hard;
The gentle overcomes the rigid.
(In Stephen Mitchell, *Tao Te Ching: A New English Version*.)

FACT FILE

Worldwide Numbers

There are some 20,000 Daoist priests and several million followers of Daoism, mostly in China.

Holy Symbol

The main symbol of Daoism is the yin and yang, which represents the balance of power between two forces. Yin is a cool dark force that is said to be present in clouds and winter and yang is a hot bright force that is seen in the earth and summer.

Holy Places

Many Daoist temples are centers of local pilgrimage. Special significance is given to five major mountains in China: Tai Shan, Song Shan, Hua Shan, Heng Shan Bei, and Heng Shan Nan.

Holy Writings

The *Daodejing* is the most important text. Many Daoists believe that it was written by Laozi, but others argue that it was written by more than one person. The *Daodejing* consists of philosophy and poetry explaining the way of the Dao and the universe. It also gives advice on how to live life. It was compiled in the fourth century B.C.E.

Founders

There have been many figures throughout history which have been seen as founders of popular Daoism, most importantly Laozi of the sixth century B.C.E. and Zhuangzi of the fourth century B.C.E.

Festivals

Daoists celebrate the birthday of important ancestors and heavenly deities, and the solstices. They also celebrate the major Chinese festivals. These include the Chinese New Year (January/ February); the Hungry Ghosts Festival (August); and the Lantern Festival (September/October).

BIBLIOGRAPHY

Chai, Ch'u, and Wineberg Chai, *The Story of Chinese Philosophy*. New York: Washington Square Press, 1961.

Clayre, Alasdair, *The Heart of the Dragon*. Boston: Houghton Mifflin, 1984.

Cleary, Thomas, *Vitality, Energy, Spirit: A Taoist Sourcebook*. Boston and London: Shambhala, 1991.

Coye, Molly Joel and Jon Livingston, eds., *China, Yesterday and Today*, translated by Cyril Birch. New York: Bantam Books, 1989.

Liu, Wuji, and Irvin Yucheng Lo, *Sunflower Splendor: Three Thousand Years of Chinese Poetry*. Bloomington: Indiana University Press, 1975.

Mitchell, Stephen, *Tao Te Ching: A New English Version, with Foreword and Notes*. New York: Harper and Row, Publishers, 1988.

Palmer, Martin, *The Book of Chuang Tzu*. London, Penguin Classics, 2006.

Yutang, Lin. *The Importance of Living*. New York: William Morrow, 1998.

FURTHER READING

Capra, Fritjof, *The Tao of Physics,* 4th ed. Boston: Shambhala, 2000.

Chai, Ch'u, and Winberg Chai. *The Story of Chinese Philosophy.* Westport, Conn: Greenwood Press, 1975.

Clayre, Alasdair, *The Heart of the Dragon.* Boston: Houghton Mifflin, 1986.

Dingbo, Wu, and Patrick D. Murphy, eds., *Handbook of Chinese Popular Culture.* Westport, Conn. and London: Greenwood Publishing Group, 1994.

Dreher, Diane, *The Tao of Inner Peace,* rev. ed. New York: Plume, 2000.

Dyer, Wayne, W., *Change Your Thoughts—Change Your Life: Living the Wisdom of the Tao.* Carlsbad: Hay House, 2007.

Hoff, Benjamin, and Ernest H. Shepard. *The Tao of Pooh ; The Te of Piglet.* New York, N.Y.: One Spirit, 2003.

Kirkland, R., *Taoism: The Enduring Tradition.* New York: Routeledge 2004.

Kohn, Livia. *Daoism and Chinese Culture.* Cambridge, Mass: Three Pines Press, 2004.

Little, Stephen, and Shawn Eichman. *Taoism and the Arts of China.* Chicago: Art Institute of Chicago, 2000.

Paper, Jordan D., and Laurence G. Thompson. *The Chinese Way in Religion.* The Religious life in history series. Belmont, CA: Wadsworth Pub. Co, 1998.

Pregadio, Fabrizio. *The Encyclopedia of Taoism.* London: Routedge, 2008.

Robinet, Isabelle, and Phyllis Brooks. *Taoism: Growth of a Religion.* Stanford, Calif: Stanford University Press, 1997.

Thompson, Laurence G. *Chinese Religion: An Introduction.* Belmont: Wadsworth Pub. Co, 1996.

Wong, Eva. *Teachings of the Tao: Readings from the Taoist Spiritual Tradition.* Boston: Shambhala, 1997.

WEB SITES

Further facts and figures, history, and current status of the religion can be found on the following Web sites:

http://www.tao.org
The Center of Traditional Taoist Studies maintains an authoritative online resource to promote Daoist ideas and practices.

http://www.religioustolerance.org/taoism.htm
An overview of Daoism and its history.

http://www.taopage.org
Teachings on Daoism and related topics such as yin and yang, meditation, and the *Yijing.* Includes online courses.

http://www.bbc.co.uk/religion/religions/taoism
A guide to the religious philosophy of Daoism, including history, spiritual practices, ethics, and martial arts.

GLOSSARY

alchemy—A philosophy, blending science, magic, and religion, in which practitioners attempted to turn common materials into gold. *See also* ELIXIR OF LIFE; SPIRITUAL ALCHEMY.

ba xian—The Eight Immortals; Daoist gods, formerly historical figures and heroes, who could be called on to help people in need.

calligraphy—The art of fine handwriting. In China, the writing of Chinese characters by hand with a fine brush; also in China, considered a branch of the art of painting.

Dao (Tao)—Literally, the Way; the nameless force behind all things.

Daocracy—A state or community organized around the Daoist religion.

Daodejing (Tao Te Ching)—The Laozi, the Book of the Way and Its Power; the basic writings of Daoism, attributed to Laozi.

Dao jia—Daoist thought; the essential philosophy of Daoism.

Dao jiao—The religion of Daoism.

Daozang (Dao Ts'ang)—The Daoist canon, or sacred writings.

elixir of life—In early Daoism, a "golden potion" that would ensure immortality, or eternal life. *See also* ALCHEMY.

ghost money—A paper-printed representation of money symbolizing family wealth, designed to be burned as an offering to the gods.

heavenly worthy—A celestial being, either god or immortal; one of the Three Pure Ones, the gods of heaven, earth, and human beings.

immortal—A person who achieved perfection and rose to the Highest Purity Heaven of the Daoists, spiritually as well as physically. *See also* XIAN.

jiao—Literally, an offering; a basic Daoist ritual, simple or elaborate, conducted for many reasons but primarily for the welfare of living people.

jing—Literally, vitality; associated with creativity and the basic functions of the body including procreation. In Daoism, one of the three treasures of human life. *See also* QI; SHEN.

libation—A liquid, usually wine, poured as an offering in a religious ceremony.

libationer—An early Daoist priest.

Mao Shan—Mount Mao, site of the birth of the Highest Purity sect or the Mao Shan school of Daoism.

oratory—A place of Daoist worship overseen by a priest called a libationer.

qi—Literally, the breath of life; physical energy, the essence of life, control of which is essential for longevity and for harmony with Dao. In Daoism, one of the three treasures of human life. *See also* JING; SHEN.

Quanzhen—The Complete Reality movement, a school of Daoism marked by a return to the natural and free way of life in early Daoism.

shen—Literally, spirit, or that part of a human being that controls thought, intellect, and spirituality. In Daoism, one of the three treasures of human life. *See also* JING; QI.

spiritual alchemy—The blending of body, mind, and spirit through meditation and the practice of good health to achieve longevity.

Taijiquan—A system of exercise developed by Daoists to help people channel the flow of qi, or energy, within their bodies during meditation; often shortened to Taiji. *See also* QI.

Three Pure Ones—Heavenly deities, the three highest gods of Daoism, who together embody all aspects of the Dao.

Way of the Celestial Masters—Tian Shi, the Daoist sect established by Zhang Daoling, the founder of religious Daoism.

wuwei—The Daoist philosophy of "nondoing"; the practice of being aligned with nature.

xian—The state of immortality. *See* IMMORTAL.

yin and yang—In Chinese philosophy, the inseparable opposing forces of the universe, whose balance creates harmony. Yin is dark, female, quiet; yang is light, male, active. One cannot exist without the other.

zi—Literally, master or teacher; a title of respect.

INDEX

ABOUT THE AUTHOR

The late **Paula R. Hartz** was a teacher and a textbook editor, and specialized in writing nonfiction and educational materials for elementary and secondary school students. She is the author of *Baha'i Faith, Native American Religions, Shinto, Daoism,* and *Zoroastrianism,* all from Chelsea House's World Religions series.

ABOUT THE SERIES EDITORS

Martin Palmer is the founder of ICOREC (International Consultancy on Religion, Education, and Culture) in 1983 and is the secretary-general of the Alliance of Religions and Conservation (ARC). He is the author of many books on world religions.

Joanne O'Brien has an M.A. degree in Theology and has written a range of educational and general reference books on religion and contemporary culture. She is co-author, with Martin Palmer and Elizabeth Breuilly, of *Religions of the World* and *Festivals of the World* published by Facts On File Inc.

PICTURE CREDITS